PROPOSAL WRITING

SAGE HUMAN SERVICES GUIDES, VOLUME 63

SAGE HUMAN SERVICES GUIDES

A series of books edited by ARMAND LAUFFER and CHARLES D. GARVIN. Published in cooperation with the University of Michigan School of Social Work and other organizations.

A **SAGE** HUMAN SERVICES GUIDE **63**

PROPOSAL WRITING

Soraya M. COLEY
Cynthia A. SCHEINBERG

With contributions by Armand Lauffer

Published in cooperation with the University of Michigan School of Social Work

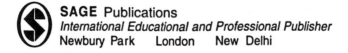

SAGE Publications
International Educational and Professional Publisher
Newbury Park   London   New Delhi

For information address:

SAGE Publications, Inc.
2455 Teller Road
Newbury Park, California 91320
E-mail: order@sagepub.com

SAGE Publications Ltd.
6 Bonhill Street
London EC2A 4PU
United Kingdom

SAGE Publications India Pvt. Ltd.
M-32 Market
Greater Kailash I
New Delhi 110 048 India

Printed in the United States of America

Library of Congress Cataloging-in-Publication Data

Coley, Soroya M.
    Proposal writing in the human services / Soroya M. Coley, Cynthia A. Scheinberg.
        p.   cm. — (Sage human services guides ; 63)
    "Published in cooperation with the University of Michigan School of Social Work."
    Includes bibliographical references.
    ISBN 0-8039-3232-4
    1. Proposal writing in the social sciences. 2. Social service. I. Scheinberg, Cynthia A. II. University of Michigan. School of Social work. III. Title. IV. Series: Sage human services guides ; v. 63.
HV41.C548   1990
658.15'224—dc20   90-19505
                                                                        CIP

98   99   00   15   14

Sage Production Editor: Susan McElroy

TO
*Ron Coley, my husband, who
supported me in all stages of this book;
and who had faith when I faltered,
praise and inspiration when I doubted,
and love and friendship always.*

—S.C.

and
*My grandmother, Virginia DeSalvo;
my parents, Lu and Norm Trinkle;
and my daughters, Rebecca and
Rachel, for their love and support.*

—C.S.

CONTENTS

FOREWORD

A few weeks ago, I was notified of an award for a project that I was convinced needed doing. The award came from a foundation that has as great a stake in the project's success as I do, perhaps more. Mine was not an exceptionally well written proposal. Another version of the proposal, submitted to the same funding source a year earlier, had been much better written. That proposal had been turned down. More accurately, it had been returned for clarification. I'd redone it and resubmitted it only to have it returned a second time. With two strikes, I figured, I had better aim my presentation more effectively the third time.

The point is that good writing and finding the right sponsor is no guarantee of funding. Effective proposals require targeted communication. The first version of my proposal had not been properly targeted. I had tried to do three things with it: (1) speak to the interests of the foundation; (2) present a rationale and an operational plan that would be acceptable to my host organization (within which the project would be lodged); and (3) address the interests of other cooperating organizations. In retrospect, I did one more thing. I tried to educate the funder by introducing new concepts that I hoped might induce the funder to see the problem addressed in the same way I saw it. Big mistake!

I should have known better. After all, I've written a great many proposals; I have even published a number of books on grantsmanship, fundraising, social marketing, and community organizing. The point is that any of us can get carried away with our sense of importance, with a conviction that the way we perceive things is not only correct but should be so perceived by others. Our advocacy for certain populations, programs, and ideas can blind us to the interests or perception of others.

In the following chapters, Soraya Coley and Cynthia Scheinberg do an excellent job in walking you through the process of proposal development and design. They will help you assess the funding environment within which your organization will have to cut a path, pointing out that what you chose to communicate with one party is not necessarily what should be communicated with another. For example, a local agency and a state public welfare agency with which it contracts to provide placement services need not have identical goals or even define the problem addressed in the same manner. It only matters that the goals pursued and the means employed by each partner be complimentary.

Chapters 4 through 9 provide you with clear and concrete guidelines on how to say what needs to be said in a proposal. They include step-by-step directives on defining needs or problems to be addressed; specifying goals and objectives; describing anticipated activities; developing an evaluation plan; spelling out the budget; and justifying the plan in terms of agency capability and the significance of the issues addressed or methods used. But what they say about the *how* of proposal writing still has to be tempered by your judgement of *what* should be said, *how much,* and *to whom.* What the funding source needed to hear from me was different than what my colleagues at work needed to know. The other agencies with which the proposed project would be interdependent had still other needs to know.

Proposal writing, and what goes on before, during, and after submission, are all part of a professional process of *communication.* Communication implies bringing together; it requires sharing what we have or could have in *common.* Communication, in its fullest sense, is a reciprocal process. A well-written proposal is based on an understanding of this reciprocity. It presumes that the party or parties being communicated with have a set of interests and concerns. The proposal speaks to those interests. It further presumes a response. If the proposal is properly phrased and targeted, the response is likely to be positive, often expressed in the form of a grant or contract award.

The award itself is a form of communication, one that demands a response in terms of action and reporting, and often in terms of shared planning and decision making. That may seem like a heavy load to impose on a single document. To the contrary, it is a much more modest load than inexperienced proposal writers (and old-timers like myself) are sometimes likely to impose on a proposal. The point is that no proposal should be expected to say everything that could be said. It only needs to say as much as is necessary at a particular point in the exchange or communication process between funders and petitioners.

With these thoughts in mind, I invite you to share an adventure with the authors and your colleagues. Proposal writing, like any form of communication, can open up new avenues of exploration that will lead to new and important discoveries . . . about ourselves, about our programs, and those with whom we work on the behalf of people in need.

—*Armand Lauffer*
The University of Michigan

PREFACE

This book is written primarily for beginning and moderately-experienced grantwriters; those who are thrust into the marketplace to compete for resources, with only on-the-job and learn-as-you-go training in proposal writing. In our work with both public and private human service agencies, we repeatedly heard the need for a guide on conceptualizing *and* writing grants. We hope our response to that need is useful, and supports the efforts of those who are seeking the resources to improve the human condition!

Computer failure, major surgery, lost data, a move from California to Virginia, guaranteed overnight mail delivery arriving two days later, and missed deadlines might have deterred some from completing this book. However, perseverance, determination, friendship, and humor were hallmarks of this process.

Writing is such a solitary, isolating activity; but there were many who were waiting to encourage and nurture us whenever we emerged from our "monastic" existence. They included Gerald Corey, who ignited the "spark" of the idea to write the book; Jerry Wright, Mikel Garcia, Corinne Wood, Judith Ramirez, Michael Russell, Judith-Annette Milburn, Wayne Untereiner, Joyce Beckett, Linda White, Barbara Henley, and Jean Acker. The support of Dr. Jewel Plummer Cobb, President, and Dr. Mary Kay Tetreault, Dean, California State University Fullerton is also acknowledged.

Similarly, we derived inspiration from our students in our proposal writing classes at California State University, Fullerton. Their repeated requests for a comprehensive guide to planning and writing grants kept us motivated.

We owe a special expression of appreciation to Carol Amato and Wrise Booker, who always made the time for critiquing and editing. We thank Terry Hendrix at Sage for initially exploring the idea of the book with us, and Armand Lauffer, for his generous patience and invaluable critiques.

THE GRANTWRITER'S PLEA

Grant me the courage
*   to write and submit a grant,*
the serenity to deal with the
*   denial of the grant,*
the wisdom to know whether to
*   revise and resubmit the grant . . .*
Please Grant Me A Grant!!!
                    —S. Coley & C. Scheinberg

Chapter 1

THE PERSONAL SIDE OF PROPOSAL WRITING

CHAPTER HIGHLIGHTS

- Definition of Terms
- The Art of Grantwriting
- Getting Organized

DEFINITION OF TERMS

In its simplest terms, a *grant* is a sum of money given to an agency or individual to address a problem or need in the community. A *contract* is a legal agreement that specifies the services to be provided and the results expected in exchange for resources. (A more in-depth technical discussion about the differences between grants and contracts is presented in Chapter 3.) The written document that is prepared to apply for funding is called a *proposal*. The individual who prepares the proposal is called a proposal writer. Proposal writing includes the entire process of assessing the nature of the problem, developing solutions or programs to solve or contribute to solving the problem, and translating those into proposal format.

Proposal writing is both an art (in capturing the essence or purpose behind the proposed service) and a science (in translating that purpose into costs, the structure of services, evaluation components, and the like). Much time and energy go into this process, and this book is designed to assist you in preparing the proposal, from conceptualizing the project to writing with technical clarity.

A proposal is a persuasive presentation for the receipt of resources. View it as an agency marketing tool. It represents what the agency intends to do in the community and provides an image to the funder of the agency. You are expected to portray the strengths and capabilities of the agency in an exciting, creative, and innovative manner.

Throughout the pages of this book, we will share the personal side of proposal writing with you to make your writing experience less painful and more fruitful. Increasingly complex community problems and a growing need for services have created a new awareness that cooperative efforts among agencies are necessary to meet those needs. In addition, as financial resources become more scarce, an urgency exists for programs of exceptional quality.

Because grant writing is an art, it is seldom, if ever, articulated. Many options are open to you as the grantwriter, from defining and understanding the problems to determining the actual services provided. You bring personal life experiences to play in the mixing pot of proposal ideas; therefore it is beneficial to consider the impact these perceptions may have on the proposal. When you become open to new possibilities, new ways of thinking, and new ways of addressing a problem, your proposal can be vitally responsive to the community it seeks to serve.

Fifty percent of the proposals funded are resubmissions that were denied the first time. This statement is not made to discourage you, but rather to ground you in the reality of the process. Because this is a highly competitive business, grantwriters must learn not to take rejection personally. In fact, too much personal investment in the proposal can work to your disadvantage, as you may lose the objectivity needed to negotiate the proposal, make modifications, or even learn from mistakes.

Throughout this book, we will bring a perspective of program development that will assist you in creatively dealing with the myriad possibilities that exist, and ultimately, that will assist in reaching logical and realistic determinations about what the best approach will be. In fact, if we can be successful in helping individuals understand the process of proposal writing in both its technical and creative form, we will have reached our goal.

PREPARING TO WRITE

The following section is dedicated to the beginning proposal writer and addresses some of the issues associated with general organization and work habits. Individuals who have written proposals before will be very aware of the usual obstacles and barriers that greet the writer along the way. As most proposals are written under the pressure of deadlines (which are almost always too short), organization becomes critical. Some keys to successful writing are listed below.

Know thyself and thy work habits

- Determine whether the proposal will be written by one individual or through a group process. If it is to be written by more than one person, delegate the data collection and writing tasks. Be sure to leave sufficient time to proofread the copy and integrate different writing styles. Try to work and accumulate everything in one location.

- Start piles of information that may be useful, such as demographic data, program ideas, articles from journals, newspaper clippings, program data, and past proposals.

- If possible, use a computer. It simplifies the writing and making corrections or moving sections around; however, a typewriter with scissors and glue will suffice.

- Establish a schedule for writing that allows frequent breaks and keeps you from having to work at all hours of the night. Announcements about submission deadlines, like the release of the RFPs (Requests for Proposals) will determine your time frame. Many government funders allow no more than four to six weeks between announcing program priorities and expecting the proposal. Some allow even less time.

- Have enough office supplies on hand: 3 × 5 cards, paper, tape, scissors, file folders, bins, paper clips, typewriter or printer ribbons, correction tape, and white-out.

Your Only Guarantees

- Your typewriter/computer will break down within 48 hours of your deadline.
- You will run out of ribbon and correction tape on a Sunday evening when all the stores are closed and the proposal must be mailed on Monday.
- You will get a cold.
- The copier will break down within 24 hours of your deadline.
- You will make some mistakes.
- Materials essential for next day delivery will arrive at least two days late.

OVERCOMING WRITING BLOCKS

There are as many ways to deal with writing blocks as there are writers, and most writers talk about their own special technique or trick to help themselves write. When you write a proposal, however, you do not have time to let writing blocks stand in your way! If you are feeling blocked in your writing efforts, consider the following:

- Do not be overwhelmed by the big proposal; take it piece by piece.
- Outline sections before writing.
- Brainstorm about the content of each section with others.
- Tell yourself that you are a prolific writer and the words will come easily.
- Begin writing on the section that seems easiest.
- Don't try to write the perfect, final draft in the first writing.
- Give yourself regular breaks.
- Verbalize your "stuck-ness" and get angry about it. Follow this up with "What I am trying to say is . . ." and write it.

Writing blocks can occur when you do not have a clear picture of the entire task. The following chapters will assist you in conceptualizing, organizing materials, and outlining the sections before writing.

Chapter 2

CONCEPTUALIZING PROPOSAL IDEAS

CHAPTER HIGHLIGHTS

* Grant Application Format
* Step-by-Step Proposal Development Process
* The Proposal from the Community, Agency, and Funder's Perspective

OVERVIEW OF THE PROPOSAL

The following items are included as standard format in most grant applications. In general, an application includes:

(1) *Cover letter, title page, and abstract.* Introduces the project and the agency to the funder.

(2) *A needs/problem statement.* Describes the community to be served and the problem or need being addressed by the proposal.

(3) *Project description.* Includes goals and objectives and provides details about the service delivery plan.

(4) *Evaluation plan.* Explains the measurement procedures to determine if goals and objectives have been met.

(5) *Budget request.* Itemizes expenditures of the project and provides rationale.

(6) *Applicant capability.* Demonstrates applicant's past performance and ability to accomplish proposed project. Describes agency structure, including board of directors, staff, and volunteers.

(7) *Future funding plans.* Indicates the plans for the continuation of the project beyond the requested funding period.

(8) *Community support.* Reflects the nature of support for the proposed project from other service providers, clients, potential service recipients, and community leaders.

Some funders may require a different format or may specify the length of each section. Always follow the funder's guidelines when they are provided.

CONCEPTUALIZATION PROCESS: NINE STEPS

If you don't know where you are going
Any road will get you there.
Alice in Wonderland

Whether you are a first-time grantwriter or seasoned veteran, conceptualizing any proposal requires thought and effort. Approaching the writing of the proposal as boring work will not do; it is fundamentally important that you view this entire process as an opportunity to serve the community and meet the needs in as comprehensive, intelligent, and innovative way as possible. Vision and courage are two words rarely invoked in books about grant writing, yet they are required attributes of the exceptional program designer. The funding climate of the 1990s will be ripe for those who stand on the leading edge of social service program design and demonstrate a calculated willingness to take risks and be creative in solving social problems. What this requires is a willingness to approach the problem with an open mind and the capability to hold, consider, and evaluate an entire spectrum of information.

Grants are written in circles, or at least so it seems, because each part ties into the other parts to eventually create a whole proposal. Consequently, it is virtually impossible to begin writing a grant proposal until you have a sense of the whole. This often makes grant writing difficult. The following discussion will assist you to conceptualize the proposal idea and begin developing it into a proposal format (see Table 2.1).

Nine Steps to Proposal Development

   (1) Understand the problem

   (2) Brainstorm solutions

   (3) Identify solutions

   (4) Describe expected results and benefits

   (5) Determine tasks to accomplish solutions

   (6) Estimate resources needed

   (7) Reassess viability of solutions

   (8) Reassess expected benefits

   (9) Identify measurement of outcomes

TABLE 2.1 Proposal Conceptualization Worksheet

Understand the Problem		Brainstorm Solutions	Identify Solutions	Indicate Expected Results and Benefits	Tasks to Accomplish Solution

Resources Needed		Reassessment of Solutions	Reassessment of Results/Benefits	Outcome Measures
Personnel	Nonpersonnel			

STEP 1: UNDERSTAND THE PROBLEM

First you must develop a clear sense of the needs/problem you are addressing in the community through this proposal. Identify the problem in terms of client circumstances or conditions requiring action and resulting from a lack of knowledge or skills, or a particular social difficulty or situation. Understand everything possible about the problem through the review of data, information, and assessment of contributing factors and root causes. Answer the questions "What is the problem? Why is this a problem? Who is experiencing this problem?" (See Chapter 4 for a detailed treatment of the problem/needs statement.)

STEP 2: BRAINSTORM SOLUTIONS

Begin the process of developing solutions from a somewhat idealistic perspective. To be successful, strive to develop these rather intangible skills: listening, observing, sensing community enthusiasm and support, and trusting your own intuition related to the viability of program ideas. Give yourself the freedom to think and create without limitations. Dream of what might be possible, of what might be done to affect the problem significantly, and what could be done in an ideal situation to create change and positive results. Do not limit yourself to thinking only about how the problem has been addressed to date.

Look for any underlying or unifying messages in these program dreams; perhaps one or two basic concepts are repeated in several of your proposed solutions. Talk to other people about their ideas to solve the particular problem, and keep looking not only for new and unique program offerings, but for the underlying themes uniting the program ideas. What real, human needs are these ideas addressing? Several underlying themes of need may exist.

As you begin to develop solutions, you must also have a sense of the agency, the community, and the funders, as well as current technology in the field. The following three subsections will assist you in further understanding the interrelationship of these perspectives on the proposal idea. Continue working on the solution from the ideal perspective outlined above and at the same time begin grounding yourself, using some of the practical considerations emerging from these sectors. It is helpful to think of the agency, the community, and the funder as a mirror. As you hold the proposal up to each of these sectors, different aspects of the program will be reflected to you, influencing and shaping the proposal as it unfolds.

Agency Perspective

Every agency's purpose is expressed in a mission or purpose statement and reflected to the community through the types of programs it provides. Usually the mission statement is fairly broad or global in nature, identifying the major issue the agency focuses on and a basic philosophy of how it is to address it. The mission statement is dynamic; it changes over time to adapt to emerging needs in the community. The mission or purpose statement is developed by the board of directors of the agency (in voluntary agencies) or by other governing bodies (in public agencies), which create policy statements framing the agency's scope and its general approach to the broad problem. Voluntary boards and public bodies can provide the auspices for new programs.

Most agencies have paid staff who turn the legislative or the board's vision and less concrete ideas into viable programs that accomplish the agency's mission. The executive director is responsible for developing the agency's services and implementing them in the community. The executive director is also the link between the auspice providers and the staff; therefore, it is vital that you work closely with the director or other administrative staff to develop the proposal idea.

Reviewing the agency purpose, its past and current programs, and its future directions is useful at this phase of proposal conceptualization. The following provides a format to examine the agency, to know what currently exists in the agency and why. This information is invaluable to moving the agency forward with consistency and balance.

Survey of the Agency
- History and mission statement of the agency
- Service area of the agency (geographic area)
- Population served by the agency (clients)
- Current programs
- Current staffing of the agency (e.g., qualifications, workload, interests, relationships)
- Future plans for the agency (What does the agency see itself doing five years from now?)
- Funding sources (percent of total budget of each)
- Other agencies providing similar services

Viewing the agency from a perspective of overall service direction provides you with the opportunity to see how program components connect with each other. Usually some overlap or dovetailing of one program with another occurs, as illustrated in the following example:

The agency may provide programs in the schools for youth and separate programs for parents in the evening. Although the services are provided to two distinct populations (youth and parents) the agency can use the school contacts to reach parents, and the parent contacts to reach into new schools. The programs are mutually beneficial to each other.

This type of interprogram relationship is desirable in most instances as it efficiently uses the agency's human resources (its staff and volunteers) and community contacts. As a result, a mutual interdependency of program efforts develops. This keeps staff in touch with each other as part of a team striving to reach a larger goal, and provides for integrated services. If the new program does not exactly "fit" anywhere in the current agency structure, you must ask yourself if it is appropriate for this agency to move in this direction.

This caveat does not automatically preclude an agency striking out in a new direction. It is possible to develop a program that does not utilize an agency's core technologies, yet is strategically sound. If you are dealing with issues and questions of this nature, continue to keep them in mind as you work through the remainder of this chapter.

Agency Competency

The next major consideration is whether the agency has the competency, connections, and staff capabilities to actually run the proposed program. In other words, as you develop the proposal idea, it is important that you keep in mind the capabilities of the agency's staff. (If staff capability requires upgrading, this may provide the rationale for recruiting new staff or retraining current staff, as described in the proposal narrative.) On the surface, this may seem very obvious, yet it requires some serious thought. From considering the educational backgrounds, ethnic backgrounds, experience in program provision, and other skills of the staff, you begin again to know what that agency is all about and where it can go. The new project may require new staff with different backgrounds. How will they fit into the team? The agency executive director will be concerned with this issue, and a skillful grantwriter keeps an eye on these needs throughout the process. The agency is a living organism, only as effective in the community as its staff and volunteers are content and committed. One can draw upon many examples in agencies as well as in the business sector, where the organization crumbled not from external forces, but from internal strife and conflict.

In determining agency competency to manage programs, look first at what the agency has done in the past:

(1) What types of programs has it run successfully?
(2) What kinds of programs were difficult for it to run?
(3) Where are the majority of the agency's contacts?

All agencies are at various levels of sophistication within their focus areas and your proposal must fit in at an acceptable level or provide for the necessary development to reach the new level. Consider the following example:

> An agency has been providing educational programs to youth in schools and now wants to develop after-school programs for teens. The agency does not have the community contacts with youth-serving providers and is therefore missing a major link needed to implement the new program in a new environment. The proposal must allow for the development of this new network for the program to be successful. Based on the knowledge that the agency has experience providing for youth and building other networks, the grantwriter determines that this is indeed an achievable aim for the agency.

Cooperative Programming

Cooperative programming will continue as an important facet of agency operations. The emphasis on cooperative programming is primarily in response to three areas of pressure: (1) diminishing financial resources; (2) increasing magnitude of social problems; and (3) a need to increase efficiency of service delivery and reduce service duplication. This third factor

has led to an increase in coalition building, networking and/or case management models. In some cases, political pressures have made agencies join
forces to garner the necessary political and community support to resist
external pressures.

Interagency relationships are somewhat fragile and require your awareness
and attention to further strengthen the agency position with other agencies in
the same field. You may not want to implement a program within an agency
that is currently being implemented by another agency. On the other hand,
sometimes you may wish to copy or duplicate a program because it serves a
different target group, or the agency has the technology to improve the
service, or perhaps, will just do a better job with the service. This type of
interagency competition can be healthy.

When agencies are competing within a limited geographic area for scarce
funding, competition over the same service can be lethal and may lead to a
dog-eat-dog mentality not beneficial to the client. Under these circumstances, meeting the need from a new angle or developing cooperative
programming may be the best approach, providing a win-win scenario for
the two agencies. Knowledge of the other agency's programs is necessary
not only from a program planning perspective, but from a political perspective, for if one plans to run into the other's territory, one must run with open
eyes, as most agencies will bring all their political clout to bear upon the
invader.

Community Perspective

In Step 1 of this framework, you were asked to understand the problem or
need you are seeking to address. Behind this level of need exists another level
of reality that you must address: Is this need something that the community-
at-large is ready to recognize and deal with? The answer to this question will
have great impact on the type of service provided. Think of the community
as displaying a hierarchy of needs and having a certain readiness to address
those needs. If the community is not ready to recognize certain aspects of the
problem or its solutions, you may have to focus the proposal on a level of
need that can be addressed.

Taking this line of thinking one step further, one can see over and over
again that some kind of a principle is operating within communities pushing
us into change. What happened within communities across the United States
to make it socially unacceptable to smoke? Years and years of health
education programs were targeted at the smoking population, and not until a
large number of people held similar beliefs about smoking did attitudes shift.
This is the principle of social learning. Similarly, antilittering, antipollution,
and recycling legislation would never be passed if the public were not
conscious of the need to protect the environment. Keeping this principle in

mind when designing a program is helpful. The goal you hope to achieve requires reaching a certain critical mass of support in the community. The objectives you use to reach the goal are small pieces of the picture on the road to that goal. The objectives must be acceptable and appropriate to the current thinking in the community. But support from the general public may not be enough.

The project also needs support from the clients receiving the service and from others seeing a need for the service. Assess the agency's capability to gather support in areas key to running the program. For example, if the proposed project requires the participation of the schools, can the agency get a letter of support from the school districts, the Department of Education, or the Superintendent of Schools?

Funder's Perspective

As soon as you have a sense of the proposed project, begin identifying potential funders. The availability of funds will often lead you to place more emphasis on certain aspects of the project over others. This is a normal consequence of interaction with funders. Be prepared to take advantage of opportunities for funding (even if unexpected) and at the same time, be wary of changing the focus of the project too much if it will lead the agency in the wrong direction. The worst thing a grantwriter can do is develop a project because some money is available "over here." This money-chasing approach has ruined the integrity of many agency programs and results in an agency headed in a direction other than that originally intended. The reality of the grant-writing business however, is that once you have the program idea and have found funders to support that idea, you will also look at the specific emphasis the funder places on the program. As a result, adjustments will be made in the project.

Corporate, foundation, or government funders view the proposal from several perspectives. They are concerned about whether or not the proposed project fits within the mission or guidelines that they have developed to direct their funding activities (Chapter 3 addresses the funder's perspective in detail.) Funders consider a proposal that meets their mandates for funding, that comes from an agency that has strong community support and a good reputation for getting the job done, and that will reflect on the funder in a favorable way.

STEP 3: IDENTIFY SOLUTIONS

Now that you have brainstormed several solutions, select and list the one(s) on which you wish to focus. Provide a rationale for your project selection. The following guide assists you in testing the merits of the specific proposal idea.

Guide for Identifying the Proposal Idea

___Y ___N   1. Does your program idea fit within the mission of the agency?
___Y ___N   2. Does your idea address aspects of community need?
___Y ___N   3. Can you document this need?
___Y ___N   4. Does your program idea have a well-defined target group (population who will receive this service)?
___Y ___N   5. Does this idea fit within the acceptable range of the agency? (Consider staffing, space, and experience).
___Y ___N   6. Do you know what other agencies are doing to address this need?
___Y ___N   7. Does your program idea excite the executive director of the agency?
___Y ___N   8. Will the clients use, like, "buy" this service?
___Y ___N   9. Does your program idea meet the needs of the funder? (Is it a good use of public dollars? Remember: It's your money you are spending!)
___Y ___N 10. Does your program enhance/support future agency development?

Above all, you must be sensitive to cultural differences and perceptions related to addressing the need so that the will or needs of one racial/ethnic group are never imposed or forced on another. In addition, unless services are being provided within the penal system (e.g., court-mandated services), participation in a program should never have the potential of forcing or coercing clients into the services. You can address ethical considerations in program development through the following questions:

- Is the need this program addresses recognized by the client as a need?
- Is there any chance that participants can be coerced into this program?
- Is there any chance that this program can adversely affect its target population's reputation/status in the community?
- Does this program impose particular values on the target group other than its own?

STEP 4: RESULTS/BENEFITS OF THE SOLUTION

List the results/benefits you expect to see if the solution is implemented in the population you seek to serve. Look at the benefit from the perspective of the client in terms of change in knowledge, attitudes, belief, acquisition of skills, and/or change in behavior. Change may also occur in the client's physical, economic, or social condition or in his/her environment (such as improved health care delivery services). Determine what changes will take place and what will have happened to whom as the result of each of the project's activities. Will there be a single effect or will there be multiple changes in different groups?

STEP 5: DETERMINE TASKS TO ACCOMPLISH SOLUTIONS

Identify the specific tasks or implementation activities needed to accomplish or provide the program solutions. This step is also referred to as the implementation, project activities, or methodology section, and looks at each of the steps in providing service: for example, recruitment of staff or program participants, material development, public relations activities, training sessions, workshops, and newsletters. These major tasks will be developed in conjunction with a time line later in the book. For now, list major tasks associated with preparation for service activities and the actual delivery of service.

STEP 6: ESTIMATE RESOURCES

Identify personnel and nonpersonnel resources needed to accomplish the tasks listed above (e.g., staff, volunteers, materials, equipment, and facilities). This will provide a general estimate of the program cost as it is now conceptualized.

STEP 7: REASSESS SOLUTIONS

Now that you have information on the general costs and resources the solution will require, plus a broader perspective of the tasks that need to be accomplished, do not be surprised if things change. Modify the solution accordingly or move on to consider another solution on your list. Avoid becoming discouraged; it is better to face the disappointment now than later in the process. Testing or checking the problems out with other staff may lead to new perspectives.

STEP 8: REASSESS EXPECTED BENEFITS

Reflect on the initial problem to see whether or not these solutions or activities adequately address the needs problem and lead to the desired outcome. This step is important because as adjustments are made in the proposed solution, one may get "off track" in terms of providing the appropriate service to the clients. This double check helps ensure that the solution is client-centered and meeting the identified needs problem.

STEP 9: IDENTIFY MEASUREMENTS OF OUTCOME

Some indicator must be used to prove that the result has been achieved. Identify the criteria and data collection methods for project success. For example, if in Step 4 you indicated that clients should increase their knowledge in certain areas, you must now determine a way to test if that has indeed occurred and state the type of measurement you will use. If you chose to demonstrate a percentage of knowledge change, you may consider the use of pre- and posttesting strategies for your target group, such as written and verbal techniques.

POINTERS

Take the time you need to immerse yourself completely in this part of the process. All too often people rush on to the specific sections of proposal writing without first having a clearly defined need or much in the way of solutions to offer. This results in a jumble of ideas poorly matched to the clients' needs. If you are writing in committee, brainstorm some of these ideas through as a group, especially Steps 1 through 4. Once all members of the committee have a strong sense of the overall direction of the proposal, specific tasks can be allocated to each member.

In the overall conceptualization process, it is sometimes very helpful to simply visualize a large balloon filling up with information without making any judgments or final decisions until you have all of the information you need. As each of the sections in the balloon interacts with the others and dwells in the same space, ideas will emerge that are balanced and colored by the variety of considerations. At this point, we also refer you to Lauffer's "Branching Tree," which provides a more linear and systematic problem-solving model when working with a wide range of programmatic options and possibilities (Lauffer, 1983, pp. 124-126).

Chapter 3

UNDERSTANDING THE FUNDING ENVIRONMENT

CHAPTER HIGHLIGHTS

- Steps to funding proposals through the public and private sector
- Results of a survey of 164 foundations
- Specific suggestions to strengthen proposals

AVAILABILITY OF FUNDING

Funds for nonprofit agencies are available through two major sectors: the public and the private. In the public sector, monies are raised through taxes and other revenues of government and allocated through legislation to address social issues. The private sector represents funds from businesses and individuals addressing social issues of their own choosing.

This chapter provides information on public and private funding sources, including the identification of specific sources, query procedures, application and review processes, and types of awards. (See Appendix C for other funding resource information.) In addition, it presents the findings of our national survey of 164 private foundations that provide funding for human service programs. The processes used to access public and private sources differ. Table 3.1 illustrates the general process of funding through each sector. Each of these sectors will be explored in-depth in the following sections.

GRANTS AND CONTRACTS

Before distinguishing between the public and private funding processes, it is important to differentiate between a grant and contract. They are often

TABLE 3.1 The Funding Process

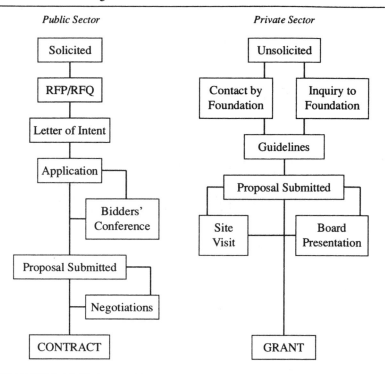

used synonymously by human service professionals. However, they have different funding purposes and arrangements. A *grant* is assistance given to an organization (or individual) to accomplish its (her/his) stated purposes and objectives. On the other hand, a *contract* represents a procurement or purchase arrangement in which the contracting agency "buys" services from the organization (or individual) to fulfill the contracting agency's obligations or responsibilities. In this case, the agency becomes an agent of the funder (Kettner & Martin, 1987). The following examples highlight the distinction:

Contract
- The state government secures employment training for recipients of public welfare aid through a contract with a private, nonprofit agency.
- The county government contracts with a nonprofit agency to provide counseling and shelter for abused and neglected children.

Grant

- A nonprofit, youth-serving agency receives a grant from a corporation to increase clients' knowledge about the dangers of drug and alcohol abuse.
- A family service agency receives funding through a foundation to expand its parent education program.

Several distinctions exist between the two funding modes. Under the contractual arrangement, the governmental bodies are legally mandated to provide services for its clients (e.g., welfare recipients, abused and neglected children). They must decide whether to provide the services directly through a public institution, or indirectly through a nonprofit or for-profit vendor. In the two examples above, they have contracted with nonprofit agencies to provide care and/or services. In these instances, those served are considered clients of the government, and the contracted agency is required to abide by all governmental mandates. Contracts are a legally binding promise to provide specified services.

In the grant aid examples, the nonprofit agencies received monies to provide services to their clients within their own policies and guidelines. Grant monies can be thought of as "awards in good faith," requiring less documentation of programmatic effort over the award term and more flexibility in daily operations.

Many of the same principles we discuss in this book apply whether seeking a grant or a contract. However, depending upon whether the purchase of service contract (POSC) reflects a partnership or market model, different emphasis may be given (Kettner & Martin, 1985).

The partnership model depicts a relationship between government and the private sector that features "the development and maintenance of the human services system. The contractual arrangements are of a joint venture nature, and are negotiated within the context of an overall concern for the stability of the human service system" (Kettner & Martin, 1985, p. 206). The market model of POSC promotes competition among potential contractors, and with all other factors being equal, the government's contracting decisions are driven by securing "the highest possible quality of service at the lowest possible cost" (Kettner & Martin, 1987, p. 36). In practice, the delivery of contracted human services is apt to include both approaches.

In some cases, whether you are preparing an application for a contract or a grant, the guidelines and format will be the same and will parallel the discussion in this book. A contract usually requires greater specificity and quantification of the amount, type, and cost of services delivered. Additionally, a contracting agency may require that a POSC work statement be prepared. (For a detailed explanation of preparing POSC work statements see Kettner & Martin, 1987; for a general discussion of POSC see Demone & Gibelman, 1989.)

PUBLIC FUNDING

Monies are available to agencies, businesses, and sometimes individuals through federal, state, and local contracts. (Research grants are available through these sources as well.) The federal and state governments announce the availability of funds through publications such as the *Federal Register, Catalog of Domestic Assistance,* and *State Contracts Register,* or directly to agencies that are on their mailing lists. Specific information in locating these publications is provided in Appendix C. Announcements of funding availability are publicized officially as a Request for Proposal (RFP), if a proposal application process, or as a Request for Quote (RFQ) or an Invitation for Bid (IFB), if a bid or purchase of service contract process.

APPLICATION INFORMATION

The RFP announces the type of programs the funder seeks to establish and clearly states the guidelines of the application process, eligibility criteria, amount of funds available, and the legislative mandate providing these funds. It is important to carefully read the RFP to determine if the funds are indeed appropriate to the project and if the agency is eligible to apply. The RFP indicates exactly how an interested party must proceed. Often one may simply call or send for an application packet or, sometimes, one responds through a letter of intent indicating a desire to participate in the funding process and giving a brief overview of the type of program to be submitted for consideration. This step enables the funder to perform an initial screening of applicants. Those passing the initial review are then invited to submit a complete proposal application.

BIDDER'S CONFERENCE

Federal, state, and local funders may also hold *bidders conferences,* designed to further familiarize the potential applicant with the goals of the funder and with specific details in proposal or bid preparation. The bidder's conference also provides grantseekers with an opportunity to learn who else is interested in submitting an application for funding. This can facilitate the exploration of cooperative proposal designs or other strategies further increasing the applicant's chance for funding.

REVIEW PROCESS

Proposals are generally reviewed by panels of professionals or experts in related fields. Usually the names of the specific reviewers will not be released by the funder; the professional backgrounds of the reviewers, however, may be revealed. This knowledge will sensitize and assist you in stating or phrasing certain aspects of the proposal in the most understandable fashion possible.

The nature of the proposal presentation varies depending on the funding entity selected. As a rule, those reviewing government proposals are professionals in selected fields related to the funding mandate. These professional consultants review the proposals from a more rigid, scientific perspective, and expect a demonstrated knowledge of the academic field and state-of-the-art practices in the proposal. The funder expects the use of technical jargon and will question the agency's competency if not used or used inappropriately.

Sections of the proposal are assigned certain point values for review. Review criteria vary from one state or federal office to another. Check your RFP for the assigned weight of each specific section.

Applications receiving a good review still may not be funded if there are more qualified applicants than money available. Frequently, reviewed applications are broken down into three categories: Approved and Funded, Approved but Not Funded, and Rejected. To be reviewed, applications must be received by the deadline and contain all of the information requested by the funder. Many federal applications provide a receipt of application with the application packet, which they will send back to you. When corresponding with state or federal funders it is wise to mail materials "return receipt requested." If proposals are not funded, applicants are typically notified regarding the reasons, and they can then use this information if they choose to resubmit in the future.

SINGLE POINTS OF CONTACT (SPOC)

Certain federal offices may require the application to undergo state governmental review. This review often requires that applicants contact their state Single Points of Contact (SPOC) early in the process to discuss their application and receive feedback at a state level. The designated Single Points of Contact person must receive a copy of the application for review.

CONTRACTS

As discussed in the beginning of this chapter, federal, state, and local proposal approval result in a contract with the applicant agency. The contract is a legally binding document for the provision of services and the accomplishment of the objectives as specified in the proposal. Prior to entering into a contract, the funder may hold contract negotiations to revise or adjust the contract. Contract negotiations are discussed in Chapter 8.

PRIVATE FUNDING

Private funding may be obtained through foundations and corporations. Unlike public funding, where legislative mandates guide the programmatic thrust and proposals are solicited to respond to them, private funders determine their funding priorities in any way they wish and do not actively solicit prospective applicants. Consequently, the private sector can support a range of programs that may be nontraditional or experimental.

Types of foundations range from those with a general or philanthropic focus to those funding programs suiting the requests of their principal donor(s). The annual report of a foundation provides specific information related to programmatic interests, funding patterns, and the application process. To locate potential funders, you can benefit from the resources in grantsmanship libraries, often located in community foundation offices and university grantsmanship centers and libraries. (See Lauffer, 1983, for assistance with developing an inventory of foundations.)

Corporations may also be involved in charitable giving programs and may allocate a certain percentage of profits to benefit human and social service programs within local communities. Grantseekers may contact the community relations office of major corporations within their community to discern if the companies have a charitable giving program. Most corporations receive so many requests for funding that a cold call probably will not result in any funding; rather, a relationship with the corporation through its employees and community relations staff is preferable.

The funder will consider a proposal for funding if it meets its funding mandates; comes from an agency with strong community support and a good reputation for getting the job done; and has the potential to reflect on the funder in a favorable way. When the program planner has discovered a way to develop services in the community that also makes the funder look good, it is a marriage made in heaven. This is true no matter who the funder is; each has an agenda that must also be met in terms of its image.

APPLICATION PROCESS

Many foundations and corporations generally accept unsolicited proposals from interested agencies and individuals four times a year. In most cases, the funder may suggest that the proposal be submitted following a standard

TABLE 3.2 Foundation Application Process (percentage)

	Required	Strongly Favored	Not Necessary
Letter from applicant	78	17	5
Initial phone inquiry	3	32	65
A standard proposal	73	18	9
Interview between foundation and applicant	17	37	46
Site visit by foundation staff	13	43	44

procedure, such as that outlined in the previous chapter. A proposal prepared for many foundations or corporations will often be much less complex than that prepared for the federal or state government. Some funders may require proposals only three to six pages in length. Typically the proposal is written in a less technical and more journalistic style.

In our survey of 164 foundations providing funding for human services, we discovered that the majority of the foundations require an initial letter of inquiry describing the proposed project. From this letter, the foundation determines whether the project idea fits into their funding mission and notifies the prospective applicant whether they desire to receive a complete proposal. In addition, nearly half of the foundations also favor an interview and a site visit prior to making a funding decision (see Table 3.2).

Sometimes it appears that more agencies are looking for money than there is money available. Certain individuals and groups of people have influence in determining how monies will be allocated. You will want to explore funding connections developed by the agency and to enlist the support of these individuals in making contacts with the funders. Many times, one well-placed proposal has a greater possibility of being funded than one scattered indiscriminately to a variety of funders. Remember that foundation and corporate development consultants may also be in contact with one another and will be aware of a proposal that has been freely scattered around, consequently reducing its chances for funding.

As reflected in our survey results, many foundations and corporations will make a site visit to the agency to meet staff, the board, and view programs. These visits help the funder get a clearer picture of the agency and provide the opportunity to view other agency programs and services as well as to clarify any aspects of the proposal not understood.

REVIEW PROCESS

The review process differs from one foundation/corporation to another. For example, large corporations and foundations generally rely on staff or consultants to review proposals and make recommendations to the board. Smaller funders may rely upon an individual, family members, or board members to perform the review and make the funding decision. It helps to think of these individuals as generalists having a good sense of many different topics, but not in-depth, specific expertise in any one area. Jargon in these proposals is not recommended, as it obscures the specifics of what you want to accomplish and leads to confusion.

Once the reviewer determines that a proposal is an appropriate project to submit for board approval, the requesting agency may be asked to present the proposal to the board of directors and answer any further questions. Corporations are likely to view proposals favorably if they meet their own internal needs or promote the corporate image in the community. When writing these proposals, be aware of the WIFM rule: What's in It for Me?; work to design a program having clear benefits to the corporation as well as the agency.

The funder will be very concerned about the history of the agency and its current status. They will ask to see a current board roster, a current financial statement, a tax-exempt letter indicating nonprofit status, and a projected budget. Funders will take a good look at the management of the agency, the current staffing, and the board of directors. To put it in perspective, a funder wants to fund an agency that will effectively use the money, will continue to grow as a result of the monies invested, and has a strong chance of continuing the program into the future without the funder's support.

OTHER FUNDING CONSIDERATIONS

In addition to a well written proposal, foundations give consideration to other factors in their decision-making process. The foundations in our survey ranked these as the top factors affecting whether an agency gets funded:

- indicates a cost-effective operation
- supports other organizations in the community
- reflects cultural sensitivity and diversity
- focuses on primary prevention of the problem
- has proven track record
- establishes new, innovative programs
- receives funding from other sources

- has previous relationship with foundation
- reputation of organization not too radical
- competent and professionally trained staff

During a Council on Foundations meeting (Highlights, 1988, p. 26), program officers noted additional organizational weaknesses adversely affecting their perception of the applicant:

- overwillingness to radically change programs to meet the foundation's guidelines
- budget problems: too much of a deficit or too large of an endowment not explained in the proposal
- organization not doing anything to help themselves financially
- too many husbands and wives on the board

COMMON WEAKNESSES IN PROPOSALS

There are various articles and books identifying weaknesses in proposals that are rejected by government agencies and private funding organizations (Townsend, 1974; Tringo, 1982). Our own survey of the foundations that provide funding for human service projects revealed that two of the most common problems are: (1) not clearly identifying and substantiating a significant problem, and (2) a lack of clarity of how monies are to be expended for project activities. Similar problems exist in requests for government funding. Table 3.3 presents our survey results of some typical problems in nonfunded proposals. The chapters that follow will illuminate ways to avoid such weaknesses and errors.

PROPOSAL SCORING

Typically, government funding agencies use a weighting system when reviewing proposals, with various weights or points assigned to each section of the proposal. The review criteria and the weighting system to be used are sometimes listed in the agency's program announcements or application packets. Foundations and corporations identify their proposal evaluation criteria through funding announcements, but are less likely to indicate the point values assigned to specific proposal sections.

In reviewing the proposal scoring criteria used by public and private funders supporting human service programs, we found they generally weighted the proposal sections in the following order:

- project approach, including goals, objectives, and project activities
- needs/problem statement
- budget
- agency capability
- evaluation

TABLE 3.3 Weaknesses in Proposals

Weaknesses	How Common in Proposals Not Funded (percentages)
Problem addressed is insignificant	44
How monies will be used is unclear	42
Nature of the problem is unclear	33
Inappropriate method of addressing the problem	31
Inadequate documentation of the problem	28
Methods do not suit the scope of the problem	28
No clear plan for evaluating the program	28
Objectives are not clearly measurable	27
Time schedule is unreasonable	21
Problem is more complex than can be addressed	20
Agency has no track record in the problem area	20
Community not involved in the planning process	16

Funders are looking for projects that are realistic, that stand a good chance of being successful, and are ambitious from two perspectives: (1) they reach out into unknown or untried arenas, which, if successful, will be a step into the future for social service agencies and a feather in the cap of the funder; and (2) they use financial resources efficiently and indicate a level of energy and commitment on the part of the agency staff. This means that people are working, and working hard at their jobs and accomplishing great things.

Funders do recognize commitment within an agency and look to get as much for their money as they can within a realistic and achievable range. The following chapters provide a guide for thinking about and preparing each proposal section in order to enhance your ability to compete successfully in the marketplace of human service resources.

Chapter 4

THE NEEDS/PROBLEM STATEMENT

CHAPTER HIGHLIGHTS

- Approaches to conceptualizing the needs/problem statement
- Types and sources of data to strengthen the needs/problem statement
- Framework for organizing and guide to writing the statement

PURPOSE OF THE NEEDS/PROBLEM STATEMENT

The needs/problem statement provides a thorough explanation of the need or problem existing in the organization or in the community for which the proposal provides a partial solution. It is rooted in factual information, such as that derived through research findings, demographic data, and other scientific data sources. The needs statement not only provides a rationale for the proposed program intervention, but demonstrates to the funder the applicant's knowledge of the big picture. As such, the needs/problem statement establishes the rationale for the proposal by clearly identifying and explaining the problems requiring attention and their causes.

CONCEPTUALIZING THE NEEDS/PROBLEM STATEMENT

The phrase *needs statement* is generally used in proposals seeking funding for programs or services, while the phrase *problem statement* usually applies to more research-oriented proposals. Grantwriters will see these terms used interchangeably in many proposals formats; therefore, we have combined their use. The term *needs assessment* refers to a specific research methodology used to document whether or not a need exists.

The needs/problem statement may be written to address specific problems of an agency such as "low productivity, poor interpersonal relationships, abuse of authority, and lack of innovation" as well as concerns related to "resource development and organization, or continuity, consistency and comprehensiveness of services" (Lauffer, 1983, p. 112). (Refer to Lauffer, 1983 for a more in-depth analysis of proposals addressing agency management or service delivery issues.) This chapter focuses on proposals written by human service agencies addressing a need/problem existing in the community.

A needs/problem statement should accomplish three primary tasks:

(1) depict the needs/problem you seek to address;
(2) describe the causes of the problem and/or the circumstances creating the need; and
(3) identify approaches or solutions to date.

The needs/problem statement examines what is happening that requires attention, attempts to explain why it is happening, and discusses what currently is being done to address it. You must thoroughly understand the significance of the needs/problem statement as it provides the very underpinnings either supporting or destroying the remainder of the proposal. The needs/problem statement is not the place to develop and propose the specific "solution" or project or to describe certain characteristics of your agency. Rather, it lays the foundation for your particular solution to emerge in the next sections of the proposal.

The needs/problem statement is typically the first part of the proposal to be written. It provides a convincing case regarding the extent and magnitude of the problem in your community, and is written within the context of those who are experiencing the problem directly and indirectly. It shows the needs/problem at a local level and is compared or contrasted with the needs/problem at a state and national level. It indicates whether the problem is getting worse, better, or staying constant, and highlights the unique aspects on the local level.

This proposal section provides an understanding of the population directly experiencing the problem, including how many people and which socioeconomic groups. The needs/problem statement considers all of the factors within the population(s) affected that either maintain or contribute to the persistence of the problem. It provides an understanding of the impact of the problem on the community as a whole and it looks at the potential that nonintervention may have in the present and the future. It shows, whenever possible, what the financial, emotional, and psychological costs of the problem are, not only to the individuals, but to the community.

In addition to demonstrating expertise in understanding the various factors associated with the problem, the needs/problem statement helps the agency tie its concern about the problem to the funder's mandate and mission. Aspects of the problem that the funder seeks to target may be highlighted over other aspects in the needs/problem statement. As you demonstrate that certain approaches or solutions have the greatest potential for success in addressing the problems, the potential may also exist to replicate your project in other areas of the state or nation, making it an attractive pilot project to many funders.

It is important to frame the needs/problem statement in such a way as to make the reality of the community stand out. All too often, pockets of serious need in a community are overlooked because they are hidden under such data as median income level or median education levels. Through the collection of data in specific areas where one knows through experience that a real need exists, one can often make a solid case for intervention. The following framework builds on the work done in Chapter 2 and assists in conceptualizing a client-centered needs/problem statement that may reveal interesting new insights into the problem.

Conceptual Framework

  Clients with "A" characteristics and background live in "B" conditions/environments and have "C" problems/needs that are caused by "D."

  Clients are blocked from solving these problems because of "E."

  This problem is related to other problems "F" and, have "G" short- and long-term impact if not addressed.

  The impact of their needs/problems on the community is "H."

  Others have addressed their needs/problems by doing "I"; the result of their interventions have been "J."

  The most promising strategy for intervention now is "K."

FINDING THE DATA

The use of data provides for a primarily objective and factual documentation of the problem. Data can inform individuals of the nature of the needs/problem and the factors contributing to it, as well as dispel preconceived ideas or misconceptions about the needs/problem. In fact, when writing the needs/problem statement, you can anticipate common misunderstandings and clear these up at the beginning of the proposal. One clear benefit of the appropriate use of data is the ability to address factors associated with the problem outside of an emotional, opinionated realm.

Qualitative data can also be collected for use in writing the needs/problem statement. Quotes from reliable, credible sources (e.g., agency directors, local community leaders, and clients) are helpful in affirming that the need exists and that intervention is warranted. In using qualitative data you can present a well-rounded case that is both objective and compassionate. Testimonials about the problem will never take the place of a solid, quantitative treatment of the problem, but used appropriately, they can be very convincing. (Federal and state funders will be generally less receptive to testimonials than corporate or foundation funders. If testimonials are used, such as letters of support, it is best to put them in an appendix. Stay in the context of the funding source.)

Developing a rational and objective needs/problem statement requires the use of supportive data. Check to see that the sources you use are up-to-date as well as reliable. Obviously you can not use all of the data you find; scrutinize it carefully to make the best possible case for your proposal. Data can be retrieved from a variety of sources as reflected in the listing below:

- program data such as evaluation results, client intake information, client and/or staff surveys, waiting lists, and service records
- journals, periodicals, newspapers, newsletters, and books
- reports and documents prepared through governmental sources: state legislatures, advisory boards, departments, offices, and commissions
- reports prepared by foundations, community groups, and other nonprofit agencies
- interviews with experts in the field
- feasibility studies or needs assessments

DATA COLLECTION CATEGORIES

The following samples of data collection categories will provide you with a guide to the kind of data useful in actually writing the statements:

- Data on the incidence of the needs/problem: whether the need has increased, decreased or remains the same. Clients' current physical, emotional, social, and/or economic status.
- Data depicting the factors contributing to or causing the problem and data on related problems.
- Data comparing the need in your target area with other cities, counties, your state, and other states.
- Data on the short- and/or long-term consequences of no intervention (including cost analysis if available).

- Data on the activities and outcomes of other organizations responding to the same or similar need.
- Data evidencing a demand for service: waiting lists, requests for service, lack of culturally appropriate services, and costs.
- Data from experts in the field, including research studies on effective intervention strategies and evaluation results.

Through the needs/problem statement, one provides a picture of the situation in the community, interweaving the data that support one's rationale for service and funding. The goal is to write a clear, comprehensive statement describing the problem in such a way that it supports the project component you seek to fund. Ideally, the needs/problem statement is comprehensive in its treatment of the problem, but not overloaded with data. What you want to achieve is:

(1) a demonstration that you have a thorough understanding of the problem;
(2) a demonstration that it is the same problem the funder seeks to address; and
(3) a demonstration that your program intervention is obviously one of the best possible choices (without blatantly stating this in the needs/problem statement!).

WRITING THE NEEDS/PROBLEM STATEMENT

At this point in the process, many grantwriters face the mounds of data in front of them with increasing anxiety. The problem now becomes one of condensing and editing the data to make a powerful statement within a limited number of pages. Drawing upon the conceptual framework presented in the earlier part of the chapter, this guide now helps you begin writing. This is just one approach to writing the needs/problem statement. Be certain to follow any specific instructions provided by the funder.

A GUIDE FOR WRITING A NEEDS/PROBLEM STATEMENT

SECTION ONE

(The problem) is experienced by (# of people) each year within the state and the nation. (The problem) is defined as _____ and is found in (provide populations affected). On a local level, (the problem) affects (# of people and specific population factors). Over the past _____ years, the problem has (improved, worsened, stayed the same) and the reason for this is _____.

Discussion

In Section One, you clearly identify the needs/problem including its incidence and the characteristics of those most affected. Such identifying information might include:

- the number of people
- ethnicity, gender, age
- language(s)
- geographic location/distribution
- family size and structure
- income level
- educational background

When writing these sections of the needs/problem statement, it is preferable to present a few pertinent facts about the problem than to overwhelm the reader with too many statistics. Note in the example above that data are effectively presented within a community context. Consider placing data in relationship to other data to strengthen your request. For example:

Fifty percent of the young people in the county do not graduate from high school.

versus

Fifty percent of the young people in the county do not graduate from high school, while there is only a 10% dropout rate in the state and 27% nationally.

In addition to providing descriptive information in relation to other reference points, the second example reflects a greater sense of urgency. Comparative data are helpful in stressing the need for immediate intervention. Note also the use of the word "only," which further highlights the magnitude of the problem on a local level. Avoid presenting data on aspects of the problem you will not be addressing in the proposed intervention, unless you are also prepared to indicate why you will not/cannot act on those aspects.

SECTION TWO

The causes of this problem are _____. The major causes of this problem on the local level appear to be _____. The local level problem differs from or is unique from the statewide data or national data in that _____.

Discussion

When discussing the causes of the problem, one of the most common mistakes grantwriters make is to fall into a pattern of circular reasoning (Kiritz, 1980). Circular reasoning occurs when one argues that the problem is the lack of service that one is proposing. For example, you may write in the needs statement:

> The problem facing many teens is that they do not have access to a teen peer support group.

After doing this, you may proceed merrily on your way in proposing teen peer support groups in solution to the problem. The above statement, however, has failed to identify the needs teens have that can be met through a peer support group and in fact, gives the idea that an absence of teen support groups is the problem! The following is an example of a needs statement that would support a proposed peer support group:

> An adolescent spends an average of _____ hours per day in contact with other teens in class, during breaks, in after-school activities and on the phone. Research indicates that teens obtain approximately _____ % of their information on drugs, sexuality, and health-related topics through their peers. From a developmental perspective, teens are moving away from parental and other adult authority and into personal authority. The need to be accepted by peers and to relate to the peer group is most pronounced at this stage of development.

Circular reasoning is not always obvious to the grantwriter, but if you keep asking yourself the question, "Why do they need 'X,' " the basic needs will emerge. In the above example, asking "Why do they need peer support groups?" would have revealed the error. Keep in mind as you write that the way you define the cause of the problem will be the way you attempt to solve it; therefore, the factors you highlight as contributing to the problem should connect with your proposed objectives and intervention strategies. For example, you may emphasize the emotional or psychological state of the client as a major cause of the problem, which will then lead you to proposing a counseling intervention. Note that if the proposed intervention fails to address the obvious, major causes, you must explain why it does not.

Causes of a problem or need that exist in an individual, family, or group may stem from many factors such as:

- lack of skills
- lack of knowledge

- debilitating attitudes
- dysfunctional behavior
- poor/deprived conditions (Lauffer, 1983)

Each of these factors should be revealed by stating the exact deficit as well as the causes of the deficit. For example, one of the causes of teen pregnancy is a lack of knowledge related to human sexuality and reproduction. This lack of knowledge is caused by limited educational opportunity through schools, misinformation through peers and the media, and a general reticence to discuss issues related to sexuality in the family and society. Each of these causes is significant to program planning and can be further developed along socioeconomic and cultural lines.

SECTION THREE

In addition to the impact that the problem has on the individual, the problem costs _____ in remediation, services, and prevention. Others affected by this problem are (tell who and in what way). The consequences of not addressing this problem are _____ and/or the benefits of addressing this problem are _____.

Discussion

As public and private funds become more restricted, agencies able to document the cost savings that intervention or prevention services will provide often have an edge with the funder. When stating the benefits or the consequences, be careful not to imply that the funder is responsible for continuation of the problem if funding is not offered.

SECTION FOUR

Several promising strategies have been developed to address the needs/problem (go through the strategies for each target population). At the local level, the problem is being focused on by (give local resources).

Discussion

Assess and discuss the current community responses to the need as being adequate and/or appropriate. As you identify effective program strategies to reach the target group, look also to the need or potential for interagency cooperation or collaboration to strengthen local service provision networks. These collaborative efforts can result in communitywide strategies to address the problem and are often favored by funders.

SECTION FIVE

Barriers to services are _____.

Discussion

Service barriers to your clients may exist that either block access or make it very difficult to access services. These barriers may be due to (Lauffer, 1983; NIMH, 1976):

* availability—services may not be provided in your community or the cost is prohibitive
* accessibility—hours of operation, transportation, eligibility criteria, may be factors
* awareness—knowledge about availability of services is needed
* acceptability—perception of staff attitudes, service setting, and sensitivity to cultural and linguistic needs, gender, age, and physical factors
* appropriateness—limited intervention strategies

Each of these factors should be addressed in the needs/problem statement in a factual manner. It is important to recognize problems in the provision of service areas and to avoid being critical of the efforts of other local agencies. Jack Shakely (1986), the President of the California Community Foundation, once remarked: "Agencies attempting to discredit other agencies in order to be funded are committing murder/suicide." It is possible to state that current service levels are inadequate without criticizing the efforts of others.

Qualitative data, such as interviews with agency staff, can yield quantitative data on the nature of the problem you could not obtain elsewhere. For example, during an interview, the executive director may tell you the agency can serve only one of every 20 eligible persons requesting service. You may use that information in the needs statement as an indication of the extent of the need beyond current service capabilities.

SECTION SIX

Based on research in the field, consideration of barriers and experience, the most promising approach for this community may be _____.

Discussion

The final step in the needs/problem statement is to provide a rationale for the services/intervention you will present in upcoming proposal sections. Do not go into programmatic details but, rather, state why support for your program is warranted. Among the factors that help to strengthen the rationale are the following:

- clearly identifies the target group
- meets a client/community need
- is cost effective
- is a novel approach
- builds upon the works of others
- uses existing resources
- promotes interagency cooperation
- fits with the funder's mandate/mission
- has the potential of being replicated

POINTERS

If possible, know who will be reviewing the proposal and/or have a copy of the legislation authorizing funding. In this way, you can get a sense of the technical language or jargon that may receive the funder's preference over other terminology. If in doubt, write the statement in a journalistic style to a well-educated, but nonspecialist, reader.

Use data with integrity. Do not manipulate or alter data, but use it selectively to make your case. If a discrepancy exists in the data, explain it and if you question the validity of certain data, omit it.

If data do not exist on the local level, or are not collected in a manner useful to this social issue, it is acceptable to point that out. The development of appropriate data collection techniques may be incorporated into one of the proposal objectives.

Do the best you can with this section and then let it go; writing a needs/problem statement is an ongoing process with always more to do and consider than one has time for. Remember to select the main points, substantiate them, and move on.

Project Description

The project description section of the proposal consists of three subsections, each with different aims:

(1) *The Goals and Objectives* subsection identifies the results or benefits expected from the project;

(2) *Project Activities* (also referred to as plan of action, methodology, work plan, implementation activities) provides a detailed account of the activities designed to accomplish the results or benefits; and

(3) *The Evaluation Plan* explains the criteria and the methods to be used for determining the results and successes of the project.

Each of these subsections will be described in the next three chapters. Although we discuss them in separate chapters, and proposal applications may also differentiate them, they are interconnected and represent the entire scope of what you desire to achieve, how it will be accomplished, and what evidence will be used to show the results.

Chapter 5

GOALS AND OBJECTIVES

CHAPTER HIGHLIGHTS

- Distinguishing Goals and Objectives
- Developing Goals
- Formulating Objectives

PROJECT GOALS

Most projects are based on one, two, or, at the most, three goals. Goals of a project represent an ideal or hoped for state. For example: The goal of a project focused on teen pregnancy prevention may be to eliminate unintended adolescent pregnancy in Grant City.

Other examples of goals are:

To provide a pollution-free environment in the United States of America.

Women in the state of Illinois shall receive early and adequate prenatal care.

To eliminate birth defects in Orange County.

As you see in these examples, goals are ambitious statements! They are the desired state of things. As such, they are not generally attainable over the short term. Lauffer (1983, p. 114) states that goals, "energize us by providing us with purpose and meaning to our efforts to respond to human needs and concerns."

Goals are usually written indicating the geographic area in which the services are to be provided. (If the geographic area has been established in the goal, it is usually not necessary to repeat it in the objective.) To write the goals for your project, return to the need or problem and state the major reasons for your work. The following questions can assist you in developing goals:

> What ideal condition will exist if we eliminate, prevent, or improve the situation?
> What is the overall, long-term condition desired for our target group(s)?

When applying for funding through federal or state sources the goals may already be developed and listed in the RFP, in which case it is advisable to simply restate those goals adding the geographic area of service. If you are developing both goals and objectives, double-check to be sure that the goals fit within legislative mandates or other funding missions.

FORMULATING OBJECTIVES

Objectives are the actions taken to attain the goal. They provide the "promise" of what will be done over the course of the project period. Objectives are specific, achievable, measurable statements about what is going to be accomplished within a certain time frame. Typically, three to four objectives are derived from each project goal. For example, with the goal "To eliminate unintended adolescent pregnancy in Grant City", one objective may be targeted to youth, another to parents, and a third to teachers, counselors, and clergy. The two major types of objectives, process and outcome, are explained below.

PROCESS OBJECTIVES

Process objectives describe the procedures or the steps to be taken toward accomplishing a desired end, but they do not indicate the impact of those steps on the client. Many times process objectives are formulated because the activities involved in implementation are important to the overall understanding of how a problem or need gets addressed. They help to provide insight into experimental, unique, and innovative approaches or techniques used in a project. Process objectives are usually designed to increase knowledge of the agency about its own system in order to improve the delivery of services.

For example, process objectives might be written for different types and amounts of staff interaction with clients, to examine outreach activities with difficult-to-reach youth, or to describe interagency collaboration. A process objective focused on coalition building is not concerned with *what* is accomplished by the coalition, but in *how* the coalition is formed and maintained.

Process objectives may be written to study program implementation methodology or to address the internal functioning and structure of an agency as in the following objectives.

Ten high school peer counseling groups will be formed by agency staff within the first six months of the project.

A computerized client charting system will be developed to track and retrieve 50% of client records by June 30, 1999.

Both examples focus on the activities required to provide service rather than the impact of those activities on the clients or patients. In contrast to process objectives, outcome objectives are used to describe the expected benefits to clients.

OUTCOME OBJECTIVES

The second and more common type of objective is known as an outcome objective. Outcome objectives specify a target group and focus on what happens to them as a result of the intervention. Outcome objectives reflect a change in: behavior, skills, attitudes/values/beliefs, knowledge, or conditions.

Well-stated objectives provide the following:

- a time frame for the service or study
- the target group of the service/study
- the number of clients to be reached
- the expected measurable results or benefits
- the geographic location or service locale; for example, group home, hospital, jail (if not in the goal)

An objective may also identify the target group in terms of their age, gender, and ethnicity (if applicable). Objectives use action verbs (reduce, increase, decrease, promote, or demonstrate) to indicate the expected change in knowledge, attitude, behavior, skills, or conditions. They define the topic area to be measured (e.g., self-esteem, nutrition, communication) and the date by which the results will be completed.

As you develop objectives, think again about the needs of the clients. Is the purpose of your project to increase client's knowledge in certain topic areas to affect behavior? Do your clients have the knowledge, yet still persist in unhealthy behavior leading you to work more directly on attitudes, values, or beliefs? What is it exactly that you hope to change? Will you focus on changing knowledge, behavior, or attitudes, values and beliefs, or on improving the conditions for a group? The objective that you write should capture the primary purpose of the service you hope to provide to the client.

Many times staff in therapeutic settings have difficulty in formulating measurable outcome objectives and are more apt to develop process objectives. Their difficulty lies in finding ways to conceptualize and make observable the progress of clients, especially those who are in nonbehaviorally oriented counseling settings, and in subjecting the client to a formal evaluation process. Thus staff often find it easier to describe the therapeutic process as an objective, without stating a quantifiable or measurable outcome objective. As funders focus greater attention upon agency accountability and efficient allocation of resources through such mechanisms as purchase of service contracts, agencies will need to increase their capacity to measure their effectiveness and impact.

The way that the objective is written will determine the type of evaluation to be conducted. For example, a knowledge-based objective may be measured using a pre- and posttest or competency test design. A behavioral-based objective may be assessed through observation, a questionnaire, interviews or other techniques, while a scale instrument might be used to assess changes in attitudes, values, and beliefs. A more in-depth discussion of evaluation techniques is in Chapter 7.

The following is an example of an outcome objective to determine a change in knowledge in the target group:

Twenty-five hundred (2,500) adolescents in county high schools will increase their knowledge about human sexuality and interpersonal relationships by 35% by June 30, 1999.

An objective developed to address behavioral change in clients at-risk for AIDS could be stated:

Two hundred (200) adults at risk for AIDS residing in the Mission Street District will reduce their risk-taking behaviors in sexual activity and drug-use by 30% by June 30, 1999.

The beginning grantwriter is apt to confuse an objective with an implementation activity. A common error is to write the actual program or service that is going to be offered. Such an error would result in the following example of a *poor* objective:

A six-week educational program on human sexuality, relationships, and decision making will be received by twenty-five hundred (2,500) adolescents in Orange County by June 30, 1999.

Why are adolescents receiving a six-week program? To increase their knowledge or skills? To change behavior? As you write your objectives, make sure you are stating the expected *outcome* of program, not the program itself.

The following example shows how a single goal can lead to several process and outcome objectives.

GOAL

To prevent drug use among young people in Grant City by promoting their educational, social, and emotional well-being.

PROCESS OBJECTIVES

* To form a coalition of ten youth-serving agencies in order to develop a comprehensive plan for providing after school activities at two junior high schools.
* To establish a multilingual teen drug prevention hotline with a corp of 100 volunteer high school students.
* To develop a multimedia drug abuse prevention campaign targeted to junior high school students and their parents.

OUTCOME OBJECTIVES

* One hundred at-risk junior high school students attending the after-school peer counseling program will increase their knowledge by 30% about the dangers of drug and alcohol use by June 30, 1999.
* One hundred and twenty-five junior high school students who are academically at-risk and participate in the after-school and weekend tutoring program will show a 30% improved competency in their reading and math scores.
* One hundred and fifty parents will increase by 60% their knowledge about effective communication techniques for teaching their children about decision making, goal setting, and the dangers and lure of drugs.

The goal statement provides a general aim and direction for the project, but lacks in specificity as to what will be achieved. The process objectives depict major activities within the context of the goal statement, but they do *not* state what the impact of those activities will be. In contrast, the outcome objectives specify *who* and *how many* are to achieve *what results*.

POINTERS

Common errors in writing objectives include: (1) putting more than one measurable outcome in the objective and (2) saying much more than is needed in the objective. Keep the objectives simple and clear. Objectives should be realistic and not promise more than can be delivered within the time stated. Remember that objectives are directly tied to the contractual relationship between the agency and the funder, and as such, the agency may be held accountable if the objective is not met. In writing objectives, you want to stretch as far as possible to make the project cost-effective and attractive to the funder, but not so far as to find the objective unattainable.

Chapter 6

PROJECT ACTIVITIES

CHAPTER HIGHLIGHTS

- Implementation Plans
- Description of Project Activities
- Timetable
- Staffing Plans

PURPOSE OF THE PROJECT ACTIVITY SECTION

The project activity section is the nuts and bolts of the proposal; it provides a clear account of what you plan to do, why you have chosen the particular approach(es), who will do it, and in what time frame the tasks will be accomplished. This section is the logical next step after writing the goals and objectives, for it explains to the funder *how* the objectives are to be attained. It presents a reasonable and coherent action plan that justifies the resources requested. The project design should generate confidence that your implementation plan reflects sound decision making and is the most feasible approach for addressing the need/problem.

CONCEPTUALIZING THE ACTIVITIES

In Chapter 2 we presented a decision-making framework for proposal development, which included making an initial determination of the tasks to accomplish the solution. In the first part of this chapter, we shall assist you in refining that list of tasks and in formulating a systematic, step-by-step project design plan for the proposal, using the Project Activities Worksheet

TABLE 6.1 Project Activities Worksheet

Project Objectives	Services Planned: _____ _____ _____		Project Evaluation
	Preparatory Activities	Implementation Activities	
What are the expected benefits/results?	What are the start-up tasks?	What activities are necessary to provide the service?	What measurements will be used to assess whether the services yielded the expected benefits and results?

(For a more in-depth discussion of project planning and implementation techniques, see Schaefer, 1985, 1987). In the second part of the chapter, we will describe how to organize and write the section.

The Project Activities Worksheet depicts the interconnection among several proposal components and assists in a more complete identification of the tasks needed, the program strategies planned, and the outcomes to be measured. The objectives serve as the foundation for developing the project methodology. The tasks and activities link directly to the objectives and provide the funder with some indication of the reasonableness and rationality of your implementation plans for achieving the desired results. Listing these activities also helps to identify major gaps in your service delivery plan.

The ability to think through all the necessary steps of a project is critical to its success, for they help to direct the staff, volunteers, and evaluators in the performance of their roles. In the middle section of the Project Activities Worksheet there are three subsections: (1) Services Planned, (2) Preparatory Activities, and (3) Implementation Activities. They reflect the main steps in planning for the delivery of services. In some instances, the same project activities may be associated with more than one objective.

SERVICES PLANNED

This subsection of the Project Activities Worksheet identifies the planned project outputs, that is, what service(s) will be offered to the target group(s).

In specifying the outputs, indicate the types and the amounts of services to be provided, and/or the products to be developed. Indicating the services planned differs from stating the project objectives in that the former refers to what is given to (and received by) the target group, while the latter describes benefits derived by or changes in the target group as a function of the services delivered. Determining outputs can also assist with project monitoring, for you can assess the extent to which you are providing the services at the level(s) proposed. The following are examples of Services Planned statements:

- 100 hours of group counseling with 75 drug abuse addicts
- 200 health care newsletters printed and distributed to persons 55 years and older
- 400 meals distributed daily to home-bound persons 65 years and older
- 150 high school dropouts, 16 to 18 years old, will receive their high school equivalency degree and complete a seven month computer training program

Stating succinctly the services to be provided assists in formulating a clear framework for identifying the activities and tasks to be accomplished.

PREPARATORY ACTIVITIES

Reflecting on the services to be offered, begin to list the preparatory activities necessary to get the project underway. These are the general tasks associated with project start-up. With each task it is also useful to identify the person responsible for accomplishing the activity and to estimate the time needed for completion. While the type of preparatory activities will vary depending upon the project, the following are typical:

- staffing plans
- site/facilities selection
- special equipment needs
- product/material development
- interagency agreements and collaboration plans
- community involvement and linkages
- outreach to target group(s)

IMPLEMENTATION ACTIVITIES

These activities relate to the service delivery process or the specific approaches to be employed with the target group to accomplish the project's objectives. In general, human services programming can be grouped into four major categories: (a) training or education, (b) information development and dissemination, (c) counseling and other support services, and (d) provision of resources. In developing a sound implementation strategy, you must have an understanding of the decisions to be made and the tasks to be performed. The following questions are designed to assist you in formulating a strategy and can be used as a decision-making checklist. Examples of the kinds of services in each category are given as well.

Training or Education. Examples: career development workshop, job preparation training, family life education

- What are the training or educational objectives?
- What will be the content of the presentation(s)?
- What strategies or techniques will be employed, including teaching aids and tools?
- Who will conduct the training?
- What will be the typical format and schedule?

Information Development and Dissemination. Examples: ad campaign for drug abuse prevention, videotape on AIDS prevention, health care newsletter, parent training manual, resource referral service

- Who is (are) the targeted group(s)?
- What will be the content and format?
- How will it be developed? Who will be responsible for development?
- What group(s) will review before distribution?
- What dissemination strategies will be employed?

Counseling and Other Support Services. Examples: bereavement counseling, support group for victims of abuse and violence, crisis hotline

- What counseling strategies or techniques will be used?
- What are the underlying assumptions or evidence of the validity of the techniques?
- What will be the counseling process and format?
- What issues and content will be addressed?
- Will others (e.g., support system, professionals) be included in the process? How?

Provision of Resources. Examples: transportation for the disabled, meals program for older Americans, youth recreation program, health care screening

- What resources will be provided?
- When and how will they be delivered?
- Who will develop, organize, and deliver them?
- Any special equipment and/or materials needed? How will these be obtained?

PROJECT EVALUATION

Evaluation is the final component of the Project Activities Worksheet. Using the project objectives and service delivery plan as a basis, indicate the methods for determining whether the outcomes are achieved. This section should answer the question "How will I determine whether the objectives have been attained?" (Chapter 7 will describe evaluation strategies and techniques.)

WRITING THE PROJECT ACTIVITIES SECTION

After conceptualizing the plan of action, it must be translated into a coherent, complete, and organized description. This section may be referred to in the proposal guidelines as the methods, program narrative, program approach and the like. Many times grantwriters are unclear as to how to proceed with the writing, for the proposal instructions do not give specific details about the content and format. The writer is left to complete it as he/she determines best. The funder's only desired outcome is a well-written and organized presentation for accomplishing the project's goals and objectives.

Experienced grantwriters typically present the project activities in a variety of formats to assure that the reviewers have a complete understanding of how the objectives will be achieved. In addition, computer-generated charts, figures, and project flow diagrams (see Schaefer, 1985, 1987) are often used to enhance the presentation. We will describe four common formats used: (1) the narrative, (2) the outline, (3) the scope of work, and (4) the time line.

THE NARRATIVE

The narrative gives the plan for achieving the objectives and provides a rationale for the selection of a particular approach. It identifies the tasks and explains how they will be completed. To ensure that there is a logical connection among the activities, it is useful to present the narrative using subject headings for sequential tasks or for project phases.

Completing the Project Activities Worksheet presented earlier in this chapter will help assure that you have given thought to the variety of details and decisions necessary before writing a coherent and rational plan of action.

Information from the Worksheet can be expanded and transferred into the appropriate sections. The following is a suggested outline that can be arranged in any sequence deemed suitable.

OUTLINE

PROJECT ACTIVITIES

I. Introduction. Begin with a brief summary of your proposed project, including a statement as to why this is the best approach for addressing the need/problem.

II. Site/Facilities Selection. Describe the project's location and whether special facilities will be needed. Give evidence of the status of those arrangements.

III. Staffing Plans. Identify your plans for staffing the project, including recruitment techniques and training activities. (In a later section, you will write job descriptions for each position.)

IV. Product and Material Development. Indicate whether special materials or products will be needed, such as training manuals. Describe what is needed, who will do it, and how they will be developed, and any plans for review or testing before use in the project.

V. Special Equipment. Describe the special equipment needs of the project and the sources from which they may be secured.

VI. Interagency Agreement and Collaboration. Explain how other agencies will be used to support the aims of the project. Be specific as to why and how they will be involved.

VII. Community Involvement. Show how the community is involved in the project, for example, advisory committees, and volunteers.

VIII. Clients/Participants. Provide a detailed description of the intended clients/participants. Among the items to consider are:

(1) their background characteristics, such as socio-demographics;
(2) a rationale for their selection, including eligibility criteria;
(3) outreach strategies, with evidence of their effectiveness;
(4) referral mechanism for other services needed but not provided by the project;
(5) procedures for obtaining client consent; and
(6) strategies for reducing client attrition.

IX. Project Approach. Use the items just provided under each category of service as a framework for describing your action plan, that is, training or education, information development and dissemination, counseling services, and provision of resources. Describe the uniqueness of your project design, provide a rationale for your course of action, and show the interrelationship of the activities.

X. Summary (if space allows). Briefly summarize your program strategies and why you think they will be effective in achieving the goals and objectives.

THE OUTLINE

Another format used for project description is the outline, which relates the activities to a specific goal and objective. It depicts a clear relationship between what is done and what is expected to be achieved. Since most projects will have multiple goals and objectives, the outline is merely extended. One can also use this format when writing a narrative description. A typical version of the outline follows:

PROJECT GOAL:
    PROJECT OBJECTIVE:
    Implementation Activities:
        1.
        2.
        3. (etc.)
    Evaluation:

SCOPE OF WORK

In addition to a narrative many state agencies require a Scope of Work Form (Figure 6.1), which provides the basis for the legal contract. Similar to the outline just depicted, this format shows the relationship between the goal, the objectives, and the activities; and it extends the presentation by also identifying the plan for evaluation. As you study the Scope of Work Form, you will notice that the goal is written across the top of the page and is numbered (for example, Goal #1). The first column contains an objective that is numbered in sequence relative to the goal for which it applies. The second column identifies the major activities that will accomplish the particular objective. It is also customary to list underneath each activity the job title of the individual(s) responsible for that activity. In the Time Line Column indicate the begin and end date for each activity. The final column is for the evaluation of the objective (not the completion of the activities). Show how each objective will be measured to determine if it has been successfully met.

TIME LINE

In addition to describing the project activities, funders typically desire to see a schedule of those activities. A visual display of the action plan provides

Contractor _____

Contract No. _____

Agency No. _____

County _____

SCOPE OF WORK

The Contractor shall work toward achieving the following goals, and will accomplish the following objectives. This shall be done by performing the specified activities and evaluating the results using the listed methods to focus on process and/or outcome.

Goal No. _____ (Specify)

MEASURABLE OBJECTIVE(S)	IMPLEMENTATION ACTIVITIES	TIMELINE	METHOD(S) OF EVALUATING PROCESS AND/OR OUTCOME OF OBJECTIVE(S)

Page_____ of_____

Figure 6.1 Scope of Work Form

the reader with a real sense of when different phases of the project will be undertaken. It also helps to generate confidence in your ability to effectively plan and carry out the grant or contract requirements.

There are a variety of techniques that can be used to present the project's timetable. One of the most common is a GANTT Chart, which shows activities in relation to a time dimension (see Table 6.2). In preparing a GANTT chart: (1) list the major activities and tasks, (2) estimate the amount of time to be expended on each activity or task, and (3) determine how the activity is spread across a time period. The time period is typically divided into months or quarters and an activity's begin and end points are depicted with row bars, Xs, or similar markings. Generally, when viewing a GANTT chart, activities are listed in the order in which they will be accomplished (a forward sequence).

By examining the GANTT chart, one sees which activities are to occur within a particular time frame, and can be useful for project monitoring. Also some funders require quarterly reports and from the GANTT chart they are able to determine what you plan to accomplish each quarter. It is wise to include the preparation of any reports to the funder as an activity on the chart. If there are few activities or the project has a relatively short time span, the following time line format may be used.

ESTIMATING TIME

Determining how much time a certain project will take is probably one of the most difficult things to do. Making a fairly accurate assessment of time will be important not only in working through the implementation activities, but in developing the budget as well. See Appendix A for a discussion on estimating time.

ORGANIZATIONAL STRUCTURE AND STAFFING

Almost every proposal application requires a description of the organizational structure and staffing plans. Typically, they are placed in the proposal appendix, unless otherwise indicated. If the proposed project is part of a larger agency structure, show the project's organizational structure and the linkages between it and the rest of the agency. An organizational chart is useful for depicting the administrative structure and lines of responsibility for project management (see Schaefer, 1987, pp. 149-168).

A brief narrative, describing the project's administrative and management procedures, should also be incorporated. Indicate whether the project will have an advisory committee or policy-making body; if so, who will comprise

TABLE 6.2 GANTT Chart

ACTIVITIES	1st Quarter	2nd Quarter	3rd Quarter	4th Quarter
I. Staffing				
Recruitment and Selection	▬			
Training	▬			
II. Instructional				
Materials Development				
Child abuse identification manual developed	▬▬			
Manual review by educators and social work professionals		▬		
Audio visual materials obtained		▬		
III. Organization of Child Abuse Prevention Workshops				
Selection of trainers	▬			
Workshop and site scheduling		▬		
Recruitment of participants		▬		
Materials duplication		▬		
Conduct workshops			▬▬▬	
IV. Project Evaluation				
Evaluation designed		▬		
Workshop evaluation conducted			▬▬▬▬	
Reports to funder				

TABLE 6.3 Time line

ACTIVITY	TIME
Hire staff	January 1—February 15
Train staff	February 15—March 15
Develop curriculum	February 1—March 15
Schedule workshops	January 20—May 15
Conduct workshops	April 20—October 30
Conduct evaluation	April 20—November 30
Prepare final report	December 1-December 31

it, how will they be selected, and what will their responsibilities be? Discuss any staff accountability measures to be used. Describe how project staff relate to other staff and functions within the agency. For example, some staff may divide their time between the project and other agency activities.

Job descriptions should be included for all key professional positions. They should give precise information on the major responsibilities and tasks of the positions. Many times they are written in vague terms, leaving personnel without a clear picture of what is expected of them. There are major advantages in developing comprehensive, concise task-based job descriptions, including: (1) they help to clarify job expectations with workers, (2) they can facilitate staff performance reviews, (3) they can provide continuity in staff turnover, and (4) they assist in monitoring the relationship between worker performance and the goals and objectives of the project (Pecora & Austin, 1987, pp. 24-25). A job description typically includes:

- definition of the position
- major responsibilities and related tasks
- knowledge and skills required for the position
- training and experience requirements

Well-written task-based job descriptions clearly state the responsibilities and activities associated with the position, provide an indication of the expected result or outcome of the task, and estimate the amount of time and energy to be expended in each responsibility area. Pecora and Austin (1987, p. 29) have identified the following steps for developing task statements:

(1) list all the various job activities or specific responsibilities of the position;
(2) divide the job into four to six major components, which become the basis of defining broad areas of responsibility;
(3) attach a percentage weighting to each of the responsibility areas and check to see that the total for combining the weighted percentages equals 100%;
(4) distribute all the major activities under each of the components or responsibility areas adding additional activities as they are identified; and
(5) use the activity statements and convert them into task statements.

Table 6.4 illustrates a sample task-based job description.

Job announcements are shorter and should include: (1) the job title, classification (if applicable), and salary range (may be open or negotiable); (2) duty location (geographic and organizational unit); (3) description of job duties; (4) minimum qualifications; (5) starting date for the position; (6) application procedures; and (7) closing date for receipt of application.

TABLE 6.4 Modified Sample of Task-Based Job Description

POSITION DESCRIPTION FOR A MENTAL HEALTH SPECIALIST II
ADULT OUTPATIENT SERVICES

Definition of Position

Under the agency's policies and professional requirements this outpatient therapist position provides direct management of assigned clients, engages in consulting and informational activities for the community and other professional disciplines, participates in program evaluation procedures, professional record keeping, makes referrals to other local and state facilities, and works under the direct supervision of the coordinator of adult outpatient services.

Major Responsibilities and Related Tasks

I. Direct Clinical Services (70%)

1. Establishes initial data of a potential client's presenting problems, mental status, treatment history, medical problems, and assesses client diagnostically according to the best professional standards and agency policy in order to determine treatment modalities, assignment priorities, and/or provide information and make appropriate referrals to other treatment resources in the community.
2. Implements crisis or precrisis intervention procedures with potentially suicidal, homicidal, or gravely disabled clients in order to prevent destabilization, enhance adaptive functioning, and move clients toward an appropriate treatment program.

II. Client Information System (20%)

1. Establishes appropriate professional files in order to demonstrate psychotherapeutic work to agency and the state.
2. Provides necessary client information to other agencies or health care providers in order to coordinate services to identified clients.

III. Enhance Adult Outpatient Team Functioning (10%)

(and so on)

Knowledge and Skills

Activities are governed by a professional code of ethics and rules of confidentiality; thorough knowledge of the techniques and principles of psychological, behavioral, and social disorders; skill in dealing with the public in advocating for mentally and emotionally disturbed, developmentally disabled, and drug dependent persons.

Training and Experience

Must have at least a master's degree in a mental health related discipline from an accredited college or university and at least two years appropriate experience in the direct treatment of mentally ill clients under the supervision of a mental health professional.

SOURCE: Adapted from Pecora & Austin (1987, pp. 21-23).

POINTERS

The exact format of this proposal section will vary, depending upon the funder's guidelines. In general, keep in mind that the reviewer is looking for a well-reasoned plan with a realistic timetable. The Project Activities Worksheet, which assists in project conceptualization, can be shared with others to ensure that the major project tasks have been identified before you begin the writing task. As you develop this section, continue to reflect on whether the activities will lead to the expected outcome.

Chapter 7

EVALUATION PLAN

CHAPTER HIGHLIGHTS

- Process and Outcome Evaluations
- Conceptualizing the Evaluation
- Framework for Writing the Evaluation Plan

IMPORTANCE OF EVALUATION

Evaluation. The word itself can throw even the best program developer into a panic, conjuring up images of statistics, control groups, random samples, as well as other tools of evaluation. In this chapter, we will focus on the advantage of sound evaluation, for it is through the development of evaluation that is appropriate to the project's capabilities and scope, that major strides have been made in human service environments. Gone arc the days where it was simply sufficient to do "good". Now the need is urgent to both prove that good and necessary things are done (outcome evaluation) and to document how they were done (process evaluation).

Evaluation research can be used in making assessments about the merit of programs, techniques, and project materials. From a broad view, the results of such research can form the basis of position papers for lawmakers as well as the creation of advocacy groups for certain causes. Within the grant-making process, the benefits of evaluation research and data can be viewed from two perspectives: (1) the funder and (2) the agency.

FUNDER

From the perspective of the funder, the results of your evaluation may be used to:

- Determine whether the funds were used appropriately, and whether the objectives as stated in the proposal were accomplished.
- Assess if the project's benefits were worth the cost.
- Assist in the development of future funding objectives addressing the same needs/problem.
- Promote positive public relations through promotion of the benefits derived through their funded projects.

AGENCY

From the perspective of the agency, evaluation has the following benefits:

- Compels the agency to clarify program objectives so that they are measurable.
- Helps the agency to continually refine its approaches to service.
- Provides feedback on the level of effort and cost required to accomplish the tasks so that adjustments may be made in the future.
- Increases the agency's capacity to meet client need through increased knowledge about the client and effective interventions.
- Assists agency to communicate benefits of service to the public and thereby increase public support.
- Assists other agencies in program development through dissemination of results.

DEVELOPING AN EVALUATION PLAN: FOUR STEPS

In most human service agencies, evaluation plans are kept fairly simple due to financial constraints, or constraints imposed by the client or environment of the project, as well as relatively limited staff expertise in evaluation methodology. Funders will sometimes provide guidelines on the evaluation design expected, or they may simply state that an assessment of the project's accomplishments is required. Read the RFP or application instructions carefully to ascertain the nature of the evaluation desired. There is an emerging trend for funders to support more extensive evaluation, such as long-term impact, which can be beneficial to program development in the future.

We have identified four steps in planning an evaluation for presentation in the proposal. These will assist you in identifying the major evaluation components and activities you need to consider before writing the proposal. Our discussion will intentionally be cursory; for a more in-depth discussion of program evaluation design and techniques, consult our references.

Step 1: Determine the evaluation questions
Step 2: Determine the types and sources of evidence needed

Step 3: Consider data analysis plans

Step 4: Identify reporting procedures

STEP 1: DETERMINE THE EVALUATION QUESTIONS

When you design an evaluation for the proposed project, remember that *you are assessing the success of the objectives.* The objectives represent the promise to the funder and the evaluation provides evidence to support that the promise was fulfilled. There are several terms associated with types of program evaluations; for example, impact, product, process, outcome, formative, and summative evaluations are just a few. In this chapter, we will focus on process (formative) and outcome evaluations (impact, summative). Each type answers a different type of evaluation question, and when used in combination, can provide a more complete picture of the manner in which the project was implemented and what was accomplished. An example of two types of evaluation questions derived from a project objective follows:

Project Objective:
100 junior high school students will increase their knowledge about the harmful effects of alcohol and drugs by 30%.

Process Evaluation Question:
What was the most effective technique for increasing junior high school students' knowledge about the harmful effects of alcohol and drugs?

Outcome Evaluation Question:
Did 100 junior high school students increase their knowledge about the harmful effects of alcohol and drugs by 30%?

Process Evaluation

Process evaluation provides an assessment of the procedures used in conducting the project. This assessment can be used as feedback information during the operation of the project to determine whether changes are warranted. The results can also be incorporated to improve the implementation of a subsequent project with a similar focus. Process evaluation provides an understanding of how you achieved the results, that is, it describes what happened, how the activities were accomplished, and at what level of effort. Conducting this type of evaluation requires close monitoring of the project and may include:

(1) assessment of client satisfaction with the project;

(2) detailed tracking of staff efforts;

(3) assessment of administrative and programmatic functions and activities; and

(4) determining project efficiency.

Such an assessment can provide information on the level of staff effort necessary to achieve certain program results, the level of outreach necessary to reach clients, and the level of client satisfaction with the agency staff, facilities, and/or program.

For example, in addition to determining whether the project was successful in increasing clients' knowledge (outcome evaluation), you are also interested in assessing the effectiveness of the different client outreach methods used (process). To undertake this latter evaluation, you would identify the outreach activities that attract clients into service, such as: flyers, public speaking, newspaper articles, directory listings, and referral through other agencies. You might then survey clients to determine which outreach strategies they responded to, as well as measure the level of effort and cost involved with each strategy.

Process evaluation questions may focus on the delivery of a particular service or they may reflect a more general assessment of the entire project operation. The following is a sample of the kinds of questions with different project foci that may guide you in formulating a process evaluation.

Training or Education Projects

(1) What is content of the training? What are the unique features of the training?

(2) How is the training conducted? What procedures, techniques, materials and products are used? What is the background of the trainer(s)? What costs are associated with the training?

(3) What is the background of individuals trained, and which training techniques are most effective with which groups?

(4) What are staff's perceptions of the quality of the training? How can it be improved? What level of effort is required to accomplish each facet of the training?

Products/Materials Development

(1) What and how are the products/materials being developed and tested?

(2) How are the products/materials disseminated?

(3) How are the products used, including how often, by whom, by how many?

(4) What are user and staff perceptions about the products/materials?

(5) What are the cost savings associated with the products/materials?

Improving Agency Operations or Procedures

(1) What is the nature of the improved operations or procedures? How do they contrast with the previous ones?

(2) What is the implementation process for the new procedures or operations?

(3) How do the new procedures or operations affect service? Contrast cost savings and level of effort between old and new.

Improving Client Conditions

   (1) What were the conditions and how do they differ now? What is the change process?

   (2) Which techniques/methods are most effective in changing/improving client conditions?

   (3) How does the change process impact agency operation, staff activities?

   (4) What are the cost savings?

Outcome Evaluation

An outcome evaluation determines the impact or the accomplishments of the project. In contrast with a process evaluation, which answers the question "How was the result achieved?" outcome evaluation focuses on "What and/or how much was achieved? and "Did the project accomplish what it intended?" This type of evaluation is typically desired by funders so they can determine exactly what was accomplished with the resources they provided. Funders sometimes refer to this as the "so what" of the project: so what happened, what was accomplished, what difference did it make?

An outcome evaluation can range in design from simply describing the change that occurred in the clients and is attributable to the project, to developing a complex design that compares the effect on clients of different strategies or techniques. In either of these cases, you are interested in the impact the project has on clients. Using the same format as with process objectives, the following will assist in developing outcome evaluation questions with different project emphases.

Training or Education

   (1) What and/or how much information or knowledge is attained by the client?

   (2) What are the changes in skill level?

   (3) How will the clients use the training or education under various circumstances?

   (4) Is there a change in behavior, attitudes, beliefs, values, or conditions as a result of the training/education?

Products/Materials Development

   (1) How effective are the products/materials? Do they achieve their intended objective(s)?

   (2) How effective are they in comparison with other products/materials used?

Improving Agency Operations or Procedures

   (1) What and/or how much improvement occurred?

   (2) What is the impact of the new procedures on the roles and functions of staff?

   (3) What are staff/client perceptions of procedures/operations?

Improving Client Conditions

  (1) What improvements/changes occurred?

  (2) What is the impact of the changes on the client group?

  (3) What is the magnitude of the change?

  (4) What is the benefit of the change on others?

STEP 2: DETERMINE THE TYPES AND SOURCES OF EVIDENCE NEEDED

As reflected in the exercises on conceptualizing the project (Chapter 2) and determining project activities (Chapter 6), you must collect evidence to indicate success/failure of the objective. The data that you collect should appropriately answer the evaluation questions. For example, if the question requires you to assess knowledge change, you may want to measure the change through standard methods such as testing (pre- and posttests), either written or verbally administered. If participants are expected to demonstrate increased skills or behavioral changes, these may be observed through role playing, exercises, assignments, and so on.

The following list highlights examples of the types of data that can be collected easily and used in an evaluation. Use the list to generate other data ideas.

Types of Data

- number of clients served
- demographic profile of clients
- length of client involvement with agency
- client satisfaction with service
- pieces of materials distributed
- client demand for service and/or product
- change in clients' behavior, knowledge, attitudes, or conditions
- client assessment of change in self
- community perception of service
- staff perception of service

Data Sources

Sources for data can include:

- agency records
- progress reports
- time allocation records
- agenda and minutes of meetings

- activity schedules, agency calendars
- telephone call slips
- visitors' logs
- written requests for service or product
- audio or videotapes
- questionnaires, interview notes, client survey forms
- standardized tests
- staff notes and documentation of role plays, observations
- client intake/exit interviews

Data Collection and Sampling Procedures

The procedures for collecting the data and selecting a sample (if applicable) must also be considered. This means determining:

(1) persons responsible for developing or selecting the evaluation tools;
(2) how the data will be collected;
(3) whether measurements will also be conducted on comparison/control group(s);
(4) procedures for assuring voluntary participation in the evaluation;
(5) safeguards for protecting client confidentiality; and
(6) sampling plans, including type of sample, and size.

Data Collection Timetable

Another dimension to weigh is when you will collect data. This should also be indicated on the project time line. When considering the timing of the measurements, think about the benefits of collecting data.

- before the project—which establishes a baseline
- during the project—which monitors progress
- after the project—when used with baseline data, can show change
- follow-up, postproject—determines long term benefits

STEP 3: CONSIDER DATA ANALYSIS PLANS

Review the evaluation plan to determine how you will represent the data. Do you want to show frequencies, percentages, rates, comparisons, and so on? Will you compare the outcomes of different client subgroups by sociodemographic characteristics, for example, gender, age, ethnicity, income levels, and/or by the amount of exposure to the project? Which statistical techniques will be most conducive to answering the evaluation questions? Review your evaluation instruments to ensure that you have included all of the variables you may need and an appropriate method to obtain the data so that you gain maximum benefit from the effort.

STEP 4: IDENTIFY REPORTING PROCEDURES

Evaluation data are usually presented to the funder on either a quarterly or semiannual basis and at the project's end. Unless the funder specifies the reporting requirements, you should decide how you will keep it apprised of the project's activities and accomplishments.

WRITING THE EVALUATION SECTION

The decisions made about the evaluation design must be incorporated into a coherent presentation. Similar to the project activities section of the proposal, funders have different expectations and requirements for writing the evaluation plan. Some will desire an elaborative narrative description, while others will request a brief outline or scope of work format. We shall discuss both formats.

NARRATIVE DESCRIPTION

If no specific instructions have been given for preparing this section, the following is a typical format. The decisions made during the conceptualization of the evaluation are now evidenced within this framework.

Outline for an Evaluation Plan

(1) Identify evaluation purpose and questions.
(2) Describe the evaluation design.
(3) Identify what will be measured.
(4) Describe the data collection plan: type of data, source of data, data collection procedures, timetable
(5) Identify sampling plan.
(6) Discuss data analysis techniques.
(7) Highlight protection of human subjects.
(8) Explain staffing and management plans for the evaluation.
(9) Identify reporting procedures.
(10) Show proposed budget.

SCOPE OF WORK/OUTLINE

In some instances, the funder will provide forms or require a brief outline of the evaluation plan. Completion of the Scope of Work Form (See Figure 6.1) or some similar format may be the only requirement for describing the plans for measuring process and outcome. This shorter representation generally entails a listing of the project objectives, implementation activities and the types of measurements of outcome/process for each objective.

OTHER EVALUATION CONSIDERATIONS

This chapter assists you in preparing an evaluation plan for the proposal to measure process and outcome objectives. There are other considerations that may not be addressed in the proposal, but should be weighed when conducting an evaluation. In examining what was accomplished (outcome), or how it was achieved (process), one might also need to evaluate the rationale or premise upon which the project was implemented. You may find that your initial understanding of the needs/problem, your perceptions of the needed solutions, your organization's capacity, and/or the community's response did not yield the expected result. Your evaluation may call into question the appropriateness of the project's goals. The goals may not fit within the community, cultural or organizational context. Such analysis and feedback can help to strengthen subsequent project planning and implementation. You may refer to the conceptual framework presented in Chapter 2 to guide you in a reassessment of the goals, objectives, and strategies.

Unless specifically stated as objectives, a project evaluation may exclude an assessment of the service delivery process and structure. Yet, unintended benefits and/or impediments to assessing the service delivery system may result from project strategies and activities. For example, in Chapter 4 one dimension in identifying the needs/problem is to consider potential service barriers, such as: availability, accessibility, awareness, acceptability, and appropriateness. Developing an evaluation plan that analyzes whether and how the project addressed these factors could reveal serendipitous benefits or unanticipated obstacles.

Assessing the linkages between staff activities and the time and funds expended can be beneficial in the resource evaluation process. One way to evaluate these elements is presented in Table 7.1. Each staff activity shows the budgeted versus actual time and dollars spent. This breakdown helps to promote efficiency through a clear analysis of the variance between the planned and actual allocation of resources. It also assists in subsequent budgeting as well as helps to determine the cost/benefit relationship among the various elements.

TABLE 7.1 Resource Evaluation

ACTIVITIES	TIME			DOLLAR EXPENDITURES		
	Budget	Actual	Percent diff.	Budget	Actual	Percent diff.
(1) Develop workshop curriculum	15 days	28 days	87%*	$3000	$6500	117%*
(2) Schedule and publicize workshops	12 days	10 days	17%	1800	1300	28%
(3) Conduct training	20 days	28 days	40*	9000	15,000	67%*

NOTE: *indicates overbudget

POINTERS

Always be aware that the evaluation can uncover indirect benefits of the project. Such information can be presented to the funder when seeking additional support and/or can be used in the development of future funding rationale.

As is the case in other phases of the project, there may be constraints on the research design. In human services, many factors go into shaping the final plan, such as client language skills, length of time with the client, client willingness to participate in the evaluation, even the volunteers' willingness to administer the evaluation. The environment in which the service is provided will also affect your ability to evaluate it. For example, if you hold a large public meeting and hope to pass out questionnaires, you will find that most people will carry them home with them, whereas if you are in a contained environment such as a classroom, you have better control on the return.

Another constraint on the evaluation is that it does take a great deal of staff time in planning, administering, and evaluating the results; in other words, it costs money. Many times evaluation is kept simple to keep overall costs down. Ethical considerations can shape the evaluation plan as well. Depending on the type of research you desire, you may need client consent to deal with issues of confidentiality or anonymity, or to obtain parental consent if asking questions of a minor. Again, it is important to keep the client's interests foremost in your mind and respect their right to privacy as you design evaluation. If you are concerned about possible ethical issues in your evaluation, check your library or a local university for research guidelines with human subjects before proceeding.

Most major universities have research departments. It is often possible for nonprofit agencies to connect with individuals who have specific expertise in evaluation and to solicit their involvement in the project. The benefits of having a professional researcher assist with the evaluation design are obvious and if at all possible, we recommend you seek that expertise if you are not familiar with evaluation methodologies.

Keep the evaluation plan within the reach of the expertise of the agency staff. The easier it is to implement and analyze the evaluation the more likely you are to be successful. Discuss the evaluation plan with the staff. Also, feedback from other professionals in direct contact with similar clients may reveal variables that you had not considered. Evaluation can be very rewarding for the agency and ultimately, for those you serve!

Chapter 8

THE BUDGET

CHAPTER HIGHLIGHTS

- Budgeting for the First-Time Grantwriter
- State, Federal, and Foundation Budget Samples
- Budget Adjustments and Amendments
- Negotiations and Subcontracts

This chapter is divided into three sections. The first differentiates three major types of budgets. The second is written for the first-time proposal writer and proceeds on a step-by-step basis through the preparation of a line-item budget. The final section discusses budget preparation for foundations and corporations, budget adjustments and amendments, contract negotiation skills, and subcontracting considerations.

TYPES OF BUDGETS

The cost of running a program is expressed in a budget. As discussed in other chapters of this book, the program and the budget are closely tied to one another; a program costs money, and the budget tells how much it will cost and how the money is to be spent. You need not be a financial wizard to develop a budget for a program; however, you will need to allow enough time to do the research to develop the budget wisely.

Budgeting for nonprofit organizations is becoming increasingly complex. Agencies are having to respond to different funders' fiscal requirements and procedures. The demands for accountability and justification of resources are requiring different ways of viewing and categorizing funds. It is no longer

TABLE 8.1 Simplified Line-Item Budget

Budget Category	Total Budget Request (in dollars)
Personnel	41,500
Supplies/Materials	15,250
Printing	7,395
Facilities	3,650
Equipment	1,650
Project Total	69,445

sufficient for agency administrators to indicate what monies are being spent *on*; they are also being asked to describe what monies are being spent *for*, that is, for what purpose or result.

There are different types of budgets. *Line-item budgets,* which are discussed in greater detail later in the chapter, are most commonly required by funders. They represent the expenditures in specific budget categories (e.g., personnel and nonpersonnel). Two other budget types, *performance* or *functional* and *program budgets* go beyond itemizing expenditures to providing information that can assist in the efficient management and allocation of financial resources. They help to provide feedback about the costs of project activities and program objectives. A brief overview of functional and program budgets follow. (See Bryce, 1987; Vinter & Kish, 1984; Wacht, 1984 for a more detailed explanation of budgeting and financial management.)

A simplified version of a line-item budget is presented in Table 8.1. A total amount is developed for each budget category. A functional or performance budget aggregates the costs of relevant line items for each function or activity. From a properly constructed functional budget, one is able to determine the costs of performing certain units of work (Lauffer, 1983).

A program budget organizes expenditures according to an agency's or project's objectives. Thus one is able to ascertain the cost differentials between objectives. This type of budget is an aggregate of a functional or performance budget that represents the costs of individual activities or functions. As discussed in Chapter 5, objectives are formulated that give direction to a project. One then delineates the activities necessary to achieve each objective. The costs of those activities associated with a given objective can be presented in a program budget. (Table 8.2 shows the interrelationship between a functional and program budget.)

To summarize, the functional budget in Table 8.2 represents the combined subtotals of the activities ($20,150 + $16,450 + $19,575 + $13,270). The

TABLE 8.2 Interrelationship Between Functional and Program Budget

Functional Budget Activities	Program Budget	
	Objective A	Objective B
	Increase knowledge about drug abuse prevention among	
	(A) Parents	(B) Teens

(1) Develop training curriculum

Line Items

Personnel	$10,000	$8,000
Supplies/Materials	5,000	4,000
Printing	3,000	3,000
Facilities	1,500	1,000
Equipment	650	450
Activity #1		
Subtotal	$20,150	$16,450

(2) Conduct parent education training

Line Items

Personnel	$15,000	
Supplies/Materials	3,500	
Printing	450	
Facilities	350	
Equipment	275	
Activity #2		
Subtotal	$19,575	

(3) Conduct teen rap groups and seminars

Line Items

Personnel		$8,500
Supplies/Materials		2,750
Printing		945
Facilities		800
Equipment		275
Activity #3		
Subtotal		$13,270

Total for Objectives	$39,725	+	$29,720	=

Project Grand Total $69,445

program budget is the total budgeted cost for Objective A ($39,725) and Objective B ($29,720). Both budgets are necessarily equaled to the line-item budget total in Table 8.1 of *$69,445*. Presenting the budgets in this manner provides an at-a-glance comparative analysis of the project's competing functions and objectives.

LINE-ITEM BUDGET PREPARATION

The most common budget format for expressing expenditures in each of these categories is a line-item budget, where each expenditure is itemized under its appropriate category. In general, costs for a project are divided into two main budget categories: personnel costs and operating expenses. Personnel costs include the salaries and benefits of the staff required to do the project as well as consultants. Operating expenses include nonpersonnel expenditures such as rent, printing, mailing, travel, telephone, utilities, and office supplies.

The project on which you are working will probably be a piece of the entire agency service picture. It will represent a percentage of the agency's total program. If this is the case, the agency will establish a fund (an account) to receive and expend the money for that particular project. The agency will also divide certain costs among the different funds it receives, usually according to the percentage that the fund represents of total agency budget. A simple way to understand this is to consider the issue of paying the rent. If there are four sources of money coming into the agency of equal amounts, the agency could charge each fund 25% of the rent. If the proposal you are writing will be the only source of income to the agency, rent would be charged at 100%.

If you are working for a large agency, these accounting practices will be well-established, and the accounting department can tell you exactly what it will cost the agency to run the program. Give the accountant or controller specific information regarding your program's use of the agency's resources. For example, estimate the number of copies you will make on the agency's copy machine during the project year, the number of pieces of mail you will send out, the cost of phone calls, and so on. In addition, if you are working for a large agency, you can rely upon in-house expertise in determining program costs, and you will have an already established salary range for employees. Plan to allow enough time for the accountant to respond to your requests to provide actual cost figures based on your projected use of resources.

If you are writing the budget for a new agency, or a very small agency, there may not be an accountant on which you can depend. There may be no predetermined salary range for the personnel you propose to hire, or no estimates of the costs of telephone or copier service. The job of writing the budget now becomes a bit more complex and you must determine what this program will cost. The remainder of this chapter is devoted to the grantwriter who has little or no support to develop the budget. How does one begin? The following discussions will take you step-by-step through determining personnel costs.

PERSONNEL COSTS

Types of Staff Needed

What kind of staff do you need to run the project? Must they be professionally trained in the field? Can student interns be used? What clerical staff are needed? Write down each type of staff person you will need.

Time Required in Each Personnel Category

Now you want to determine the amount of time that the project will require of each specific staff position. This time is often referred to as Full-Time Equivalents (FTEs) and is expressed as a decimal. "A 1.00 FTE always means that the total amount of paid service is the equivalent of one person working full time for twelve months. Any figure less than 1.00 always states the decimal *proportion* of a twelve month full-time job for which the person or persons have been employed" (Vinter & Kish, 1984, p. 367). In some cases you may see a request for the *percent of time*, which is expressed as a percentage. For example, if you are using percent of time and have a need for a half-time employee, the position would be for 50% time, or .50 FTEs. (See Appendix A for a discussion on estimating staff time.)

Determining Salaries

Determining salaries can be a difficult task. You may need to do some research into the local marketplace to see what people in comparable positions are earning. You may also get some sense of appropriate salary range in the classified ads of the local newspaper. Once you have this data, consider any special skills that may be required as well as what you think is fair reimbursement for the effort.

At this point, we also want to point out that the poverty mentality of social services is changing. In the past, social services paid notoriously little in

TABLE 8.3 Sample Personnel Budget

Personnel	FTE*	Monthly Salary Range	Total Budget Request
Executive director	.05	$2,800–3,200	$ 1,500
Project director	1.00	2,700–3,000	33,600
Hispanic educator	1.00	2,500–2,800	32,400
Clerical	.75	1,400–1,600	17,000
Subtotal personnel			84,500
Employee benefits at 18%			15,210
Total Personnel Costs			$99,710

NOTE: *The FTE is subject to change over the contract year.

return for the education and experience required to do the work. Most agencies have found that it is difficult to attract and keep top quality people in the nonprofit arena. They have had to contend with a high attrition rate that costs the agency time, service, and money over the long run. Most funders today are well aware of the need to hire excellent staff in order to run a sound program and are willing to support it.

Personnel Budget Example

In the following example, you will see how each of the staff categories have been itemized, along with an indication of the FTEs, the fixed monthly full-time salary range, and the total requested amount for a one-year period. (Note also that the FTE has an asterisk by it referring to a footnote stating: "The FTE is subject to change during the contract year." This will provide some flexibility in the contract in case there is a vacancy in the position or some other need to deviate slightly from the stated time commitment. We have found this to be a part of some state contracts but not others; be aware that it exists.)

As you see in Table 8.3, employee benefits are also included under personnel costs. It is up to the agency to determine what is included in this benefits line. At a minimum this amount will include employer contributions for federal and state governments (e.g., taxes, unemployment insurance, social security contributions). Employee benefits may also cover health and dental insurance and retirement funds. The amount of benefit is calculated as a percent of total salary.

TABLE 8.4 Sample Operating Expenses Budget

Operating Expenses

Office supplies	$ 2,400
Rent (600 sq. ft. at $1.00 per square foot × 12 mo.)	7,200
Utilities	22,400
Equipment (rental & maintenance)	4,200
Health education materials (reproduction)	1,000
Telephone	2,400
Printing	1,800
Mileage (EPA rates)	1,500
Conferences	850
Insurance (liability)	3,500
Total Operating Expenses	$27,250

OPERATING EXPENSES

Now look at the second section of the budget, which addresses operating expenses (see Table 8.4). Again, it is important to look carefully at the proposal itself and identify all of the items that will cost money. The budget categories listed are typical among project proposals. Many state and federal funders have established fixed reimbursement rates for such things as mileage, per diem, and consultants. Many will not allow for food costs in association with any training you may want to conduct. For the beginning grantwriter it may be helpful to contact the executive director of a similar type of agency for assistance with this category. Another option is to contact a local grantsmanship center or university grants department and ask for the most current reimbursement rates in your state, or the State Board of Control that fixes the rates on a yearly basis. (You might be asking, "Why don't I call the state or federal office to which I am applying for funds to get the information?" Because you will look like a beginner and your position in the eyes of the funder may be weakened. Try to discover the answers to the above questions on your own first, and if that fails, then call the funder.)

Other details in the budget will not be apparent until you reach the negotiation stage. For example, you might have $5,000 in the budget to purchase a computer and printer. During the negotiations, the funder tells you that they will not pay for the purchase of equipment, but will allow you to rent it; you can then make the necessary adjustments. Read *all* of the instructions the funder gives on preparing the budget. Most funders will state their restrictions in their application package.

TABLE 8.5 Typical Budget Format

Geta Grant Agency
Budget Request
July 1, 1994 to June 30, 1995

Personnel	FTE*	Monthly Salary Range	Total Budget Request
Executive director	.05	$2,800–3,200	$ 1,500
Project director	1.00	2,700–3,000	33,600
Hispanic educator	1.00	2,500–2,800	32,400
Clerical	.75	1,400–1,600	17,000
Subtotal personnel			84,500
Employee benefits at 18%			15,210
Total Personnel Costs			$99,710
Operating Expenses			
Office supplies			$ 2,400
Rent (600 sq. ft. at $1.00 per square foot × 12 mo.)			7,200
Utilities			2,400
Equipment (rental & maintenance)			4,200
Health education materials (reproduction)			1,000
Telephone			2,400
Printing			1,800
Mileage (EPA rates)			1,500
Conferences			850
Insurance (liability)			3,500
Total Operating Expenses			$27,250
Total Budget Request			$126,960

NOTE: *The FTE is subject to change over the contract year.

Now we combine both the personnel and operating expenses, and have a typical format for project budget requests to the state (see Table 8.5).

BUDGET JUSTIFICATIONS

In addition to writing the line-item budget, many funders want an even more detailed description of what is included on each line and how the totals per line were reached. In a budget justification, each of the lines is explained. The following is an example of a budget justification.

Personnel

Executive Director. The executive director will be responsible for the supervision of staff, a small part of community networking, and overall program management, representing .05 FTE, for a total of $1,500.

Employee benefits have been calculated at 18%, which includes FICA and Federal Withholding, SDI, State Withholding, ETF at 1% of salaries, and Health and Dental Benefits.

Continue to list other personnel in this fashion, stating what they will be responsible for and what their salaries on this grant will be.

Operating Expenses

Rent. Calculated at $1.00 per square foot times 600 square feet of space for a total of $600 per month times 12 months at $7,200.

Phone. Calculated at $200 per month times twelve months for a total of $2,400 per year.

Travel expenses. Mostly for mileage, driving to and from school sites and community meeting places for an estimated 555 miles per month at 22.5 cents per mile times 12 months for a total of $1,500. Also included in travel is $850 for transportation and per diem (at State Board of Control rates) to one major conference. The total request for travel is $2,350.

Continue to itemize budget expenses in this manner and provide as much detail as possible in each line.

OTHER BUDGETING ISSUES

Once you understand budgeting in general, you can express it in many different formats. You will find that federal or state funders provide you with specific budget forms, accompanied by several pages of explanations. Foundation or corporate funders may request a more generic line-item budget. In any case, provide complete information on all the necessary budget forms, which sometimes is easier said than done! A sample budget format for federally-funded projects is in Figures 8.1 and 8.2.

FOUNDATION AND CORPORATION BUDGETS

Some foundations and nonprofit trusts require a more simplified budget in which you indicate expense categories rather than itemizing line-by-line.

BUDGET INFORMATION — Non-Construction Programs

OMB Approval No. 0348-0044

SECTION A - BUDGET SUMMARY

| Grant Program Function or Activity (a) | Catalog of Federal Domestic Assistance Number (b) | Estimated Unobligated Funds | | New or Revised Budget | | |
		Federal (c)	Non-Federal (d)	Federal (e)	Non-Federal (f)	Total (g)
1.		$	$	$	$	$
2.						
3.						
4.						
5. TOTALS		$	$	$	$	$

SECTION B - BUDGET CATEGORIES

| 6. Object Class Categories | GRANT PROGRAM, FUNCTION OR ACTIVITY | | | | Total (5) |
	(1)	(2)	(3)	(4)	
a. Personnel	$	$	$	$	$
b. Fringe Benefits					
c. Travel					
d. Equipment					
e. Supplies					
f. Contractual					
g. Construction					
h. Other					
i. Total Direct Charges (sum of 6a - 6h)					
j. Indirect Charges					
k. TOTALS (sum of 6i and 6j)	$	$	$	$	$
7. Program Income	$	$	$	$	$

Standard Form 424A (4-88)
Prescribed by OMB Circular A-102

Figure 8.1 Budget Information Form (side 1)

SECTION C - NON-FEDERAL RESOURCES

(a) Grant Program	(b) Applicant	(c) State	(d) Other Sources	(e) TOTALS
8	$	$	$	$
9				
10				
11				
12 TOTALS (sum of lines 8 and 11)	$	$	$	$

SECTION D - FORECASTED CASH NEEDS

	Total for 1st Year	1st Quarter	2nd Quarter	3rd Quarter	4th Quarter
13 Federal	$	$	$	$	$
14 Nonfederal					
15 TOTAL (sum of lines 13 and 14)	$	$	$	$	$

SECTION E - BUDGET ESTIMATES OF FEDERAL FUNDS NEEDED FOR BALANCE OF THE PROJECT

(a) Grant Program	FUTURE FUNDING PERIODS (Years)			
	(b) First	(c) Second	(d) Third	(e) Fourth
16	$	$	$	$
17				
18				
19				
20 TOTALS (sum of lines 16-19)	$	$	$	$

SECTION F - OTHER BUDGET INFORMATION
(Attach additional Sheets if Necessary)

21 Direct Charges:	22. Indirect Charges:

23 Remarks

SF 424A (4 88) Page 2
Prescribed by OMB Circular A-102

Figure 8.2 Budget Information Form (side 2)

TABLE 8.6 Foundation or Corporate Budget

Geta Grant Clinic Budget Request

Personnel	
Executive director at 5% time	$ 1,500
Community educator at 100% time	28,000
Clerical at 50% time	8,000
Bookkeeper at 5% time	1,200
Total Salaries	$38,700
Employee Benefits	6,966
Personnel Total	$45,666
Operating Expenses	
Overhead (rent, phone, utilities)	$ 8,500
Materials development (printing, postage)	5,200
Travel and training	1,800
Equipment (projector, screen)	2,300
Contingency fund	800
Operating Expenses Total	$18,600
Total Budget Request	$64,266

The following budget (Table 8.6) places line-item categories into more general categories. This type of budget provides the agency with much more flexibility in the actual allocation of expenses, and it is usually possible for the agency to transfer funds between lines without contacting the funder.

MATCHING-FUNDS AND IN-KIND BUDGETS

When some of the costs of the project will be assumed by the agency, the agency is said to be contributing this money *in-kind,* and this portion of agency-borne expense is indicated in the budget. Some funding sources may require that the agency provide matching funds of a certain percent of the amount requested. For example, one state office offered to fund 75% of the cost of providing a case management system to pregnant and parenting teens. The applicant must provide a 25% match.

The example in Table 8.7 indicates one way to present an in-kind budget. The first column indicates the funder's portion of the total request, the second column indicates the agency's portion, and the third column indicates the total to be allocated for each item. A similar format can be used if you are writing a proposal in which the resources are coming from more than one funder. Indicate the source of the funding in each column, followed by a total funding column. These budgets can get even more complex if the funder asks

TABLE 8.7 Sample In-Kind Budget

Personnel	FTE	Funding Request	Agency In-Kind	Total Budget
Executive Director	.05	$ 1,500	$ 0	$ 1,500
Project Director	1.00	22,000	8,000	30,000
Hispanic Educator	1.00	28,000	0	28,000
Clerical	.75	0	17,000	17,000
Subtotal Personnel		$51,500	$25,000	$76,500

NOTE: Continue listing for other budget categories.

TABLE 8.8 Source of Matching Funds

Agency Budget Match

(1) Source of Match *(check one or both)*

_____ Cash   _____ In-Kind   Note: All matching funds
                                                     must be equal to or exceed the
                                                     budget amount requested and
                                                     must be program specific

(2) In-Kind Match Detail
     Provide a budget detail that indicates the source of matching funds.

Line Item	Total Value	Source of Match
Salaries	$10,000	Revenue sharing
Benefits	2,500	General fund
Office supplies	1,200	Individual gift
Total	$13,700	

(3) Cash Match Detail

Source	Amount
_____	_____
_____	_____
_____	_____

for an itemized budget of the source of matching funds. The information
requested may resemble Table 8.8.

BUDGET ADJUSTMENTS

In the line-item budget, the agency is accounting for expenses on a per line
basis. Most funders with line-item budgets do not allow the agency to transfer
funds between lines without their consent. This process of requesting a

TABLE 8.9 Sample Budget Adjustment

	Total Program Budget		
	Time (percentage)	Prior Approved Amount	Adjustment Effective 10/15/99	New Approved Total
Personnel				
Executive director	5	$ 1,500	$ 0	$ 1,500
Project director	100	22,000	+2,000	24,000
Hispanic educator	100	28,000	–2,000	26,000
Clerical	75	15,000	0	15,000
Subtotal Personnel		$66,500	$ 0	$66,500

NOTE: Continue listing expenditures and adjustments in the same manner.

transfer between lines is called a *budget adjustment*. Table 8.9 is an example of how a budget adjustment is presented. One column lists the current contract totals for the year, another indicates the amount of money you want to add or subtract from the column, and the final column indicates the new totals. With budget adjustments you are not changing the total amount that you have to work with, just reallocating the money between lines.

The adjusted budget will most often need to have a written explanation attached, which describes what has happened, on a per line basis, to necessitate the request for a change. In the explanation. you will tell the funder why there is excess money in some lines and the cause of a deficit in others. The funder will be looking for a legitimate rationale to move funds between lines.

BUDGET AMENDMENTS

If, during the course of the contract, your scope of work has been expanded or reduced, you may need to do a budget amendment reflecting this change. A simple way to think about this is: When you need to shift money and it does not alter the scope of work in any way, you write an adjustment. If something has happened to significantly alter the scope, for example, the funder has asked you to take on an additional project or activity and will provide more money, you will write an amendment. Some funders require an amendment if you are seeking to move more than $5,000 (or some other predetermined amount). Amendments are usually written using the same budget format for requesting adjustments.

CONTRACT NEGOTIATIONS

When you negotiate a contract with a funder, be most conscious of the possible domino effect that one change in program will have on the entire program and the impact it will have on the budget. Most of the time projects are designed so that the parts are interrelated and interconnected. Changing what appears to be one aspect of the project can have considerable effect on the whole.

Upon approving the proposal, some funders conduct formal contract negotiations. The negotiation is a time when you meet face-to-face, review what is going to be provided by the contract, and discuss a rationale for the implementation activities, the objectives, or perhaps even the goals. The funder may want to change an objective, increase the numbers, add a new objective, clarify certain language. Most often the funder approves the proposal for a lesser amount of money than you requested. For example, your request may have been for $175,000 but the funder allocates only $160,000.

A caveat to first-time-grantwriters: You will be very excited that you have been funded. So excited, in fact, that you may be willing to do anything just to get the money and get the project started. BE CAREFUL. You can damage your project in the negotiations. The funder has a commitment to fund the project and will want the most for their money. No one knows the project better than you. Approach the negotiations from the perspective of win-win. The funder wants a good program just as you do. Here are a few guidelines for negotiating contracts:

(1) Reread the proposal just prior to going into the negotiations. Be intimately familiar with all of it just as you were when writing it six months ago.

(2) Create an atmosphere of partnership with the contract negotiator.

(3) Take your time when you make changes. Look at the impact any change will have on other objectives.

(4) Be prepared to discuss your rationale for keeping the project as initially developed in the proposal.

(5) If the agency has not been awarded the full amount requested, prepare a new version of the proposal in advance of the meeting. This enables you to have time to rethink the budget and program, and decide what revisions you are willing to make.

(6) Remember to "Maintain your integrity." If you know that the agency cannot do the job for the amount of money offered, despite changes to make it most cost-effective, or negotiations with the funder to reshape the project, the agency will need to decide if it is worth pursuing. It is possible (and we have seen it happen) that the agency will choose to turn down the contract because accepting it would be too costly to the agency.

SUBCONTRACTING

Subcontracting means contracting with another agency to provide a portion of the service in the proposal. Your agency receives the contract and under that contract, you also have a contractual arrangement with another agency to deliver a service. The subcontracting agency is bound by the same contractual terms as the primary contractor. The primary contractor is responsible for ensuring that the subcontracting agency abides by the terms of the contract and usually prepares a legally binding agreement with the subcontractor. (For a more in-depth treatment of the topic of contracts and subcontracting, see Kettner and Martin, 1987.) If you are utilizing subcontractors, you have to address this issue within the body of the grant itself in order to clearly identify by objectives, the role of the subcontractor in the contract, and to establish the credibility of the subcontractor in the applicant capability section.

POINTERS

As you review the steps in budget preparation, you can see why this should not be left to the last minute. Preparing the budget requires that you have a thorough grasp of the project, including all of the details of the implementation activities, so that you can be certain not to omit any major costs. *Changes in the program will have an impact on the budget, and changes in the budget will have an impact on the program.*

Chapter 9

AGENCY CAPABILITY

CHAPTER HIGHLIGHTS

- Establishing Agency Credibility
- Identifying Unique Contributions
- Reflecting Community Recognition and Support

PURPOSE OF THE AGENCY CAPABILITY STATEMENT

The agency capability statement establishes an organization's credibility to successfully undertake the project. It indicates who is applying for the grant, what qualifies an agency to conduct the project, and what resources (e.g., organizational, community) are available to support the effort. This section helps to generate confidence that the agency is programmatically competent and qualified to address the needs/problem, and is fiscally sound and responsible.

IMAGING THE AGENCY

In developing this section, the grantwriter must reflect the agency's image of itself as well as the constituency's image of it. This includes describing the organization's unique contributions to those they serve and capturing the community's regard for these contributions. When preparing this section, one should provide quantitative evidence of the agency's accomplishments. A recurring weakness found in this section of the proposal is making only qualitative assessments of the organization without some corroborating data to support the claims.

Depending upon the funder's guidelines, the content of the presentation may vary and might be placed in the introduction, project description, or in a separate section of the proposal. A capability statement should accomplish two things: (1) it should describe the agency's characteristics and its track record; and (2) it should demonstrate how those qualities make them qualified to undertake the proposed project. Many times grantwriters accomplish the first task but leave it up to the reviewers to infer the latter. They often fail to present a cogent argument that connects what they have done with what they are now proposing to do.

A typical agency capability statement will reflect much of the following information:

Mission of the agency. The overall philosophy and aims of the organization.

History of the agency. A brief overview of when, why, and how the agency started, and whether its focus has changed over time.

Organizational resources. A description of the agency's funding track record, including other grants received, and the human and material resources available to the organization (including the pertinent background of staff, especially their expertise in areas that respond to the needs/problem, other professionals associated with the agency, any special equipment, materials, and services that can support the proposed project).

Community recognition and support. An indication of how the agency is regarded, including awards, accreditations, and honors bestowed upon it and the staff, as well as how the community is involved in the agency's operation and structure (e.g., through membership, in programs, on committees, and boards).

Interagency collaboration and linkages. A depiction of the linkages and support available from other organizations that can assist with the proposed project, including memberships in local, state, and national networks and bodies.

Agency programs. An overview of the unique programmatic contributions the agency makes to its clients and the community, including the aims and types of programs, and a quantitative picture of what is accomplished (e.g., the numbers served, the distribution rate of materials, the cost savings).

Agency strengths. A description of the organizational characteristics that make the agency particularly suited to implement the project. In general, you indicate what is being proposed and how that fits with what the organization already has accomplished. For example, the agency may already be serving the target group, or addressing the needs/problem, or using a particular technique or strategy that it now wishes to modify or implement in a different manner.

SUPPORTIVE DOCUMENTATION

Depending upon the funder, you may be expected to provide documentation on the agency's capability. Place these materials in the appendix. They should not be lengthy testimonials. Be selective in the type of documentation you incorporate into the proposal. Typical examples include:

- Letters of cooperation from other organizations and/or professionals indicating their support of the proposed project, as well as their willingness to be involved in its implementation.
- Letters from professionals attesting to the merits of the agency and the proposed project.
- Letters from the agency's constituency (such as clients indicating the importance of this project to them and others in similar situations).
- A summary of agency accomplishments including awards, and recognitions from local, state, and national groups.
- A listing with qualifications of board members and other key advisors or consultants.

REQUESTING LETTERS OF SUPPORT

Most agencies send a letter specifically requesting support for a particular project. Typically, you provide a brief synopsis of the proposed program, the funding source you are applying to, and specific instructions for writing the letter, as well as to whom the letter should be addressed, and whether to mail it to your agency or the funder. Table 9.1 is a sample of a request for a letter of support to other organizations.

As the grantwriter, be prepared to make follow-up phone calls to the agencies and to pick up the letter if you are nearing the proposal deadline. In some instances you may be asked by the organizations to draft a letter of support for them. This is often ideal as you can be very specific about the items you want emphasized by each supporting source.

POINTERS

Sometimes the agency capability section is used as the introduction to the proposal. When writing this section, avoid overusing the words *we* and *our*. It is appropriate to refer to the name of the agency or simply say the agency throughout the text. Write as if you are developing a public relations article for a national newsletter, informing the reader, making it interesting, but keeping it brief.

TABLE 9.1 Letter of Support Sample

WE NEED YOUR SUPPORT

The Geta Grant Agency is applying for funding to the State Department of Education to provide child abuse prevention services to the parents of K-6th grade students in the Smart School District. As you are aware, child abuse continues to be a major problem in our community with a 15% increase in the number of reported cases in the last two years. Some social welfare professionals and educators in our community have estimated that 50% of the families in the Smart School District are at-risk for perpetuating abusive behavior. The need to provide alternatives is greater than ever. Geta Grant's program will assist parents in:

(1) recognizing problem behavior
(2) developing new coping strategies
(3) increasing parenting skills
(4) becoming aware of community resources for people in crisis

Your letter will be instrumental in the funder-review process. Please help us by affirming the need for this program and by indicating your possible willingness to be involved in the project. Please address the letter to: _____, but mail it to me for inclusion in the proposal, no later than 5 p.m., April 2, 1999. Thank you for your support!

Chapter 10

FUTURE FUNDING

CHAPTER HIGHLIGHTS

- Income-Generating Projects
- Community/Corporate Partnerships
- Envisioning the Project in the Future

CONTINUATION FUNDING

Do you plan to continue this project in the future? If so, how do you plan to fund it?

These are questions that almost all funders ask. In the majority of cases, the answer to the first question will be yes followed by a brief description of how the program may be developed in the future, what major changes may occur in program format or what new opportunities may be on the horizon. The answer to the second question may be much more problematic for the grantwriter. Human nature being what it is, we are more likely to have fixed our minds on obtaining the initial funding for the project rather than concerning ourselves with funding of the project beyond the current request. From this mind-set one is likely to feel very put upon, frustrated, exasperated, and downright angry when confronted with this question. "How would I know, do you think I have a crystal ball??!!" This may be what you are thinking, but it is *not* the answer to the question.

Viewing the question from the funder's perspective provides you with the rationale needed to proceed. It is nice to support projects that will do wonderful things over the course of the funding, but rather frustrating to find that they simply cease when your funds are no longer available. As a funder you know that you cannot support the project forever. Consequently you begin to look for projects that have the potential to continue the work even after your funds are expended. You seek a project that is an investment in the future.

How do you go about developing future funding plans? The following discussion leads you through a process to develop these plans. The rewards of such planning are great, for you will see the strengths and weaknesses of your project in terms of fundability, marketability, and life-expectancy. Do not be surprised if, again, this process reshapes the project in its current form and leads you to emphasize certain aspects of the project over others.

DETERMINING INCOME-GENERATING POTENTIAL OF THE PROJECT

You will want to begin by asking yourself several questions to ascertain if the project has the potential to generate income.

- Can you charge a fee-for-service to your clients?
- Is it possible to market products or materials developed under the project?
- What kind of fee structure must begin immediately to meet this goal?
- How would products or materials be marketed?

In reality, most human service programs have the potential to generate some income through the services they provide. However, many clients are unable to pay the full cost of services and therefore must be subsidized. Future funding plans typically include multifunding sources, which combine the income the project can generate through service and material fees, as well as grants and contracts through public and private sources.

THE LIFE CYCLE OF A PROJECT

What happens when you forecast the project over a five-year period? This perspective is very useful for seeing yet unrecognized potential for the project. Consider the project now as having three stages.

Stage One. There is a total reliance upon public and private funds as you develop and implement the project.

Stage Two. You may have some income as a result of implementing a fee-for-service structure or product, some grant money, and some community organization involvement providing volunteers.

Stage Three. The program reaches self-sufficiency and is utilized as a base upon which to develop future programs and funding.

Can it be done? The following suggestions may help with future funding plans.

MULTISOURCE FUNDING

Consider if perhaps there is a way to tie the service into other markets over the course of the funding so as to develop greater revenues in the future. For example, let us suppose that the service you provide can also be of benefit to individuals in the workplace. Can you build a plan into the initial proposal that enables you to develop these relationships and this potential so that at the end of the initial funding there is an opportunity for corporate support? Can the project be provided in a marketplace that can pay full fees and in this way subsidize low-income participants?

Perhaps it is also possible to broaden the project's staffing to include volunteers from other organizations in the future. Is this a project that can attract the support of community organizations? For example, suppose that the project is parent education. You may know of a number of community groups interested in providing parent education. You approach them for funding in the future and program support in terms of implementation. This gives the community group the opportunity to accomplish its goals without spending its time developing a program and gives you the opportunity to guide the project to fuller utilization in the community. What is the possibility that another organization can come into the project and take all or part of it, as their own special project for a given period?

Obtaining underwriting for project components becomes another important source of funding for nonprofit agencies. Many agencies provide space in their materials for advertising and product promotions. Are there corporations or other businesses that want to reach the same target group you reach? Are you comfortable with the inclusion of private advertising with your materials? What would your guidelines be?

In addition to advertising in newsletters or other materials, companies will often "sponsor" program components for the positive public relations they can generate. Are there pieces of your project that can be adopted by corporations and continued into the future, such as awards or recognition banquets, training components, printing costs, or other time-specific, limited efforts?

POINTERS

As a general rule, funders will not want more than one to two pages about what you envision in the future. If it is possible to have a commitment or at least the interest of corporations or community groups in perpetuating the project beyond its initial phase, include this in this section. Sometimes funders require you to charge a fee-for-service to your clients (the federal government, for example); if so, include this projection in the budget section as well.

Write the section with confidence and optimism. Assess the income earning potential as realistically as you can. Present the direction(s) in which you will move to make the project self-sustaining, or at least more self-sufficient over time, while at the same time highlighting the sound programmatic rationale behind these moves. It may be beneficial to include a time line of future funding plans if there are several phases to their development. Any time you have an extended vision of the project with a reasonable plan for future operations, the funder will be much more secure in investing in your current efforts.

Chapter 11

ABSTRACT, TITLE PAGE, AND COVER LETTER

CHAPTER HIGHLIGHTS

- Summarizing the Project
- Letter of Transmittal
- Choosing a Title

PROPOSAL ABSTRACT

The abstract is usually written after the other sections because it gives an overview of the entire project. Unless the funder provides other instructions or forms, the abstract is usually no longer than one page. The abstract is used by the funder to initially screen for appropriateness of the proposal in light of their funding objectives. A glance at the abstract also assists staff in disseminating the document to the proper review committees or funding offices. Once a proposal is funded, the abstract is often used by funders to convey to the public their funding decisions and activities.

Although it is sometimes hurriedly written at the end, care and attention should be given to its content. This is *not* the proposal introduction, but rather, it is a complete summary of the entire project. As such, the abstract should parallel the major sections of the proposal. Typically, an abstract will:

(1) Identify the agency requesting the funds, and describe the agency's expertise and interest in the project.
(2) Summarize the needs/problem statement, highlighting data that show the magnitude, or extent, of the problem.
(3) Provide a synopsis of the project objectives.

(4) Describe the major features and components of the project.

(5) Outline the evaluation plan.   ,

(6) Provide an amount requested figure, along with a statement that summarizes the expected results/benefits.

TITLE AND TITLE PAGE

Develop a title that reflects the major goal(s) of the project. While one may develop a catchy title, its meaning should be readily understood by the reviewers. A descriptive subtitle might be used to clarify. Avoid long titles, or ones that are overused. A title page usually accompanies the proposal. Federal and state agencies will often provide the facesheets necessary (see Figure 11.1). While there is no standard format for the title page, the following is typical:

The Project Title
The Name of the Agency Submitting Grant
Agency Address
Name of Prospective Funder
Project Begin and End Dates
Amount Requested

COVER LETTER

A letter of transmittal on agency stationery, signed by the appropriate organizational official should be prepared. The letter conveys interest in the funder's mandate and mission, and states how the project fits with them. The letter should be brief (usually one page); it should indicate the agency's board approval of the proposal; it should include the contact person, with telephone number; and it should convey the willingness to respond to any questions about the project. A paragraph that summarizes the project is written as well. Remember that the letter is often the first contact between the agency requesting funds and the prospective funder. Set a tone of professionalism and competency, and the ability to be results-oriented.

APPLICATION FOR FEDERAL ASSISTANCE		OMB Approval No. 0348-0043	
	2. DATE SUBMITTED	Applicant Identifier	

1. TYPE OF SUBMISSION:

Application	Preapplication
☐ Construction	☐ Construction
☐ Non-Construction	☐ Non-Construction

3. DATE RECEIVED BY STATE	State Application Identifier
4. DATE RECEIVED BY FEDERAL AGENCY	Federal Identifier

5. APPLICANT INFORMATION

Legal Name:	Organizational Unit:
Address (give city, county, state, and zip code):	Name and telephone number of the person to be contacted on matters involving this application (give area code)

6. EMPLOYER IDENTIFICATION NUMBER (EIN):

☐☐ — ☐☐☐☐☐☐☐

8. TYPE OF APPLICATION:

☐ New   ☐ Continuation   ☐ Revision

If Revision, enter appropriate letter(s) in box(es): ☐ ☐

A. Increase Award   B. Decrease Award   C. Increase Duration

D. Decrease Duration   Other (specify):

7. TYPE OF APPLICANT: (enter appropriate letter in box) ☐

A. State	H. Independent School Dist.
B. County	I. State Controlled Institution of Higher Learning
C. Municipal	J. Private University
D. Township	K. Indian Tribe
E. Interstate	L. Individual
F. Intermunicipal	M. Profit Organization
G. Special District	N. Other (Specify) _____

9. NAME OF FEDERAL AGENCY:

10. CATALOG OF FEDERAL DOMESTIC ASSISTANCE NUMBER: ☐☐ ● ☐☐

TITLE:

11. DESCRIPTIVE TITLE OF APPLICANT'S PROJECT:

12. AREAS AFFECTED BY PROJECT (cities, counties, states, etc.)

13. PROPOSED PROJECT:

Start Date	Ending Date

14. CONGRESSIONAL DISTRICTS OF:

a. Applicant	b. Project

15. ESTIMATED FUNDING:

a. Federal	$	.00
b. Applicant	$	.00
c. State	$	.00
d. Local	$	.00
e. Other	$	.00
f. Program Income	$	.00
g. TOTAL	$	.00

16. IS APPLICATION SUBJECT TO REVIEW BY STATE EXECUTIVE ORDER 12372 PROCESS?

a. ☐ YES THIS PREAPPLICATION/APPLICATION WAS MADE AVAILABLE TO THE STATE EXECUTIVE ORDER 12372 PROCESS FOR REVIEW ON

DATE _____

b. NO ☐ PROGRAM IS NOT COVERED BY E.O. 12372

☐ OR PROGRAM HAS NOT BEEN SELECTED BY STATE FOR REVIEW

17. IS THE APPLICANT DELINQUENT ON ANY FEDERAL DEBT?

☐ Yes   If "Yes," attach an explanation   ☐ No

18. TO THE BEST OF MY KNOWLEDGE AND BELIEF ALL DATA IN THIS APPLICATION/PREAPPLICATION ARE TRUE AND CORRECT. THE DOCUMENT HAS BEEN DULY AUTHORIZED BY THE GOVERNING BODY OF THE APPLICANT AND THE APPLICANT WILL COMPLY WITH THE ATTACHED ASSURANCES IF THE ASSISTANCE IS AWARDED

a. Typed Name of Authorized Representative	b. Title	Telephone number
d. Signature of Authorized Representative		e. Date Signed

Previous Editions Not Usable

Standard Form 424   REV 4-88
Prescribed by OMB Circular A-102

Figure 11.1 Facesheet for Application for Federal Assistance

The Grantwriter's Guide to National Holidays

You know it is a holiday when
    You can't get the county demographers
        on the phone for the statistics you need,
    Agency directors will call back after your
        deadline,
    The mail isn't delivered and neither are your
        support letters,
    Your staff doesn't come to work,
    All stationery stores are closed and you
        need a printer ribbon,
    The copier repair technician has an answering
        machine on,
    All of the libraries are closed, and
    THE GRANT PROPOSAL IS DUE!!!!

    P.S. If all computer lines are down, then
        it is a MAJOR holiday.

APPENDIX A: ESTIMATING TIME

In this section, we have provided for the beginning grantwriter an illustration of the process involved in calculating a staff person's time expenditure on a project. Suppose that Geta Clinic wants to provide an AIDS prevention education program in the county schools. The objective states:

> Three thousand (3,000) at-risk youth will increase their knowledge by 30% on HIV transmission and risk-reduction behaviors by June 30, 1999.

The implementation activities, with staff responsibilities, include:

Activity	Person Responsible
(1) Relationship established with schools	Project Director Community Educator
(2) Education programs developed and scheduled	Community Educator Administrative Assistant
(3) Parent Orientation Nights planned and conducted	Community Educator
(4) Two-hour educational presentation in students' regular classrooms on: the nature of HIV, the transmission of HIV, avoiding at-risk behaviors (decision-making skills, assertiveness training), halting the transmission of HIV.	Community Educator
(5) Student evaluation using pre- and posttest to indicate knowledge change.	Community Educator Administrative Assistant

Someone without any knowledge about community education might say:

> Okay, this is simple. An average class size would be 25. Divide 3,000 by 25 to find out how many actual classes you need; that equals 120 classes. Because the educator will spend two hours in each class, that is a total of 240 teaching hours. If I divide 240 hours by eight hours/day, then I need a community educator for 30 days.

The above reasoning process is *faulty* for a number of reasons. What factors need to be considered when implementing a community education program for Geta Clinic? The following discussion will provide an example of the kind of thinking through process needed to develop a more realistic estimate of the time it will take.

Access to the community. Has the clinic ever provided educational programs in the schools? How much time will it take to develop the necessary relationships with the schools to gain access? How much time will be spent scheduling programs? How much time in community relations to develop the network? Will the sensitive nature of the topic affect this development time by making it even more difficult to gain access to the classroom?

Service preparation, evaluation, and documentation. How much preparation will be required to provide the educational program in addition to the direct teaching time? Will the educator need to write the curriculum? Will he/she also need to evaluate the program's effectiveness? Grade the evaluation exams? Maintain other program records? Develop handouts for classroom use?

Geographic location. How many sites can be reached in a day? Consider the traffic patterns, distance, climate.

Ethnic, cultural, linguistic considerations. Will the clinic need educators from different ethnic backgrounds? What languages will need to be spoken? Written? Is a special knowledge required to work with this specific population(s), and if so, how much time will it take for the educator to acquire that?

Human capability. Consider what is humanly possible to require of a community educator in terms of actual teaching within a given day or week. The energy required in the classroom when the speaker is an outsider is considerably greater than when the audience is familiar with the person. Once the program has gained access to the schools, perhaps one two-hour presentation per day is all you can reasonably expect someone to do and maintain enthusiasm in the process.

Now it is time to recalculate the amount of time required from the educational staff. A full-time employee works 156 hours per month. You have determined that the educator will need to spend time developing relationships with the schools. You might estimate that it will take approximately eight hours of contact time on the phone and in-person per school that you want to reach. There are 50 high schools and therefore to contact each high school, it would entail about *400 hours.*

Calculate that it will take the educator approximately two to three weeks full time to review the materials that are available and to plan the curriculum. If portions of the curriculum need to be written and/or evaluation tools developed, it would take, you estimate, about one month. If we add that time together, it is approximately *300 hours.*

We already know that the teacher will spend 240 hours in the classroom. He/she will go to 120 different classes and you estimate that it will take 30 minutes travel time each way, so that is another 120 hours in traveling time. So the time spent in classroom presentations and travel time totals *360 hours.*

You have also calculated that it will take the educator approximately one hour per class to handle the evaluation component, which equates to another *120 hours.* You want the educator to have a minimum of ten hours per month to improve his/her skills and knowledge, to update records, attend an in-service, respond to correspondence, all of which adds up to another *120 hours.*

Finally, add the fact that due to the sensitive nature of the materials to be addressed in the classroom, the community educator will also need to be involved in making a presentation at parents' night so that they may review materials and ask questions. This will require two hours at 50 schools for another *100 hours* plus the one hour travel time for *50 hours.* There will be networking with other community groups, and involvement on task forces or committees, which take another five hours per month or *60 hours* per year.

The total number of hours involved in the Community Educator's work comes to *1,510 hours for the project year.* There are 1,872 hours in a work year. Some planners will tell you that once you have made your best time estimate, it is wise to take an additional 25%. The reasoning behind this is that it will always take more time than you think and there will inevitably be delays. In the case of the Geta Clinic, it appears that it would be wise to hire a full-time educator (100%) to reach 3,000 teens with an AIDS prevention program.

In the way that we have conceptualized the job now, the educator will spend the first four to five months preparing to teach and making contacts with the schools, and the remaining seven months of the project year providing the actual service. The factors we have included in calculating the amount of time an educator would spend to reach 3,000 teens should follow the implementation activities fairly closely. These calculations will also be needed as you determine the cost of the project. Often, as the true extent of time and effort needed is revealed, the implementation activities or the objectives may be modified to conform to budget restrictions.

APPENDIX B: SAMPLE PROPOSAL AND CRITIQUE

We have provided a sample proposal and a critique to illustrate some of the major strengths and weaknesses in proposals. The budget has been omitted because we included a detailed discussion in Chapter 8. The length of the proposal will vary according to funder requirements. Each section of the sample proposal below has a corresponding section in the critique. You will find the critique by matching the superscript numbers in the proposal with the numbers in the critique.

This critique assesses the strengths and weaknesses in the sample proposal. The types of omissions of information in the sample document often occur in actual proposals submitted for funding. While grantwriters may be concerned with brevity and page limitations, many times they omit pertinent information that could assist the reviewer in getting a clear understanding of the agency and what it is proposing.

AGENCY CAPABILITY

SAMPLE PROPOSAL INSTRUCTIONS

Establish your organization's credibility to successfully complete this project. Describe your capabilities as related specifically to this project. Summarize your agency's activities in the past that demonstrate your qualifications to conduct the proposed project.

The Geta Grant Agency was established as a result of a communitywide task force.[1,2] The mission of the agency is to eliminate unintended adolescent pregnancy in Grant City. The agency addresses its mission through the coordination and linkage of prevention efforts, the development and implementation of primary prevention services, and through the provision of resources and technical assistance.[3]

A nonprofit organization governed by a 14-member board of directors, the Geta Grant Agency was incorporated in the state of California. The agency's membership consists of parents, educators, health care providers, clergy, and other community organizations.[4] Geta Grant Agency maintains a focus on the prevention of unintended adolescent pregnancy and has a solid reputation in the community as well as in the schools.[5] It is important to the agency that the programs and materials developed and implemented are culturally and educationally appropriate. To ensure this, the agency maintains a Family Life Advisory Committee, which is representative of the community, to review all materials.

Geta Grant has provided extensive education to the community, parents, and young people about family life issues. During this previous year, 1,900 adults received information about the problem of unintended adolescent pregnancy in Grant City through our agency's speaker's bureau.[6] More than 3,500 parents received the quarterly newsletter *Our Future*.[7] Our parenting seminars were well-attended by the community.[8] The agency provided family life education sessions in juvenile detention facilities, junior and senior high schools, churches, and community centers.[9] More than 500 teachers, professionals, and paraprofessionals received educational presentations, training, and consultation by the very capable staff at Geta Grant Agency.[10] Given the agency's track record, we feel confident that we shall continue to respond to the needs of our community.[11]

AGENCY CAPABILITY CRITIQUE

(1,2) There is no indication of how long the agency has been operating, nor a clear understanding of why or how the agency was established. Some brief history of an organization is useful to prospective funders.

(3) This statement gives the mission of the agency, but is unclear as to what prevention efforts, primary prevention services, resources, and technical assistance entail. The writer is leaving it to the prospective funder to infer the agency's mission.

(4) Depending upon the strength of the agency's membership, it would enhance this section to state the number of members.

(5) What evidence exists to show that, indeed, the agency has a "solid reputation in the community?" Any recognition or honors received that would substantiate the statement?

(6) Good indication of agency's recent experience in addressing the problem.

(7) While there is quantitative data on the distribution of the newsletter, there is no description of the purpose and nature of the newsletter. It is left to the reviewer to make inferences about what the agency is doing.

(8,9) In both of these instances, the writer has missed an excellent opportunity to give some quantitative evidence of what the agency has accomplished by enumerating the number served.

(10) This is a very limited depiction of the agency's staff. There is no evidence as to the staff's professional background or their capabilities.

(11) In general, this proposal section showed little connection between what the agency has done in the past and what is now being proposed. Further, there is no substantiation of community and client support for the agency.

NEEDS/PROBLEM STATEMENT

SAMPLE PROPOSAL INSTRUCTIONS

> Describe and document why the proposed project is necessary in your community. Make the case for your proposed intervention as appropriate to affect the problem or reduce the need. Describe and indicate why the target group needs assistance.

Unintended adolescent pregnancy is occurring at an alarming rate across all socioeconomic levels. On a national scale, twelve million American teens are sexually active and one out of ten females become pregnant (Guttmacher Institute, 1981, p. 6). One fifth of premarital pregnancies occur in the first month after the initiation of sex, and half occur in the first six months. Eight in ten premarital pregnancies are unintended. If current trends continue, it is estimated that one out of ten girls who are now fourteen will become pregnant in their teens, two in ten will give birth, and three in twenty will have abortions.[12] Teens are becoming sexually active at younger ages and in greater numbers. By the age of 13, 18% of the boys and 6% of the girls living in the United States are sexually active. Between the ages of 15 to 17, nearly half of the males and one-third of the females are sexually active.

Grant City is a community where a sizable proportion of its residents are living at or below the poverty level.[13] The 1.5 million Grant City residents have a diverse racial-ethnic background, with 45% White, 20% Hispanic, 20% Black, 10% Asian, and 5% Native Americans. More than 60% of the households consist of families with two or more persons, and approximately two-fifths of the families are headed by single parents.[14]

In a national survey,[15] Grant City ranked 6th in the nation in the number of adolescent births, or 190 per thousand. The Grant City Health Agency estimates that there were 6,500 births to adolescents aged 19 and under in Grant City in 1979, and the number has been steadily increasing.[16] Race and socioeconomic status are major predictors of early childbearing (Dryfoos, 1984). However, unintended pregnancy knows no racial or economic boundaries, and although childbearing can be predicted on the basis of socioeconomic indicators, pregnancy cannot.

Adolescent pregnancy occurs for a variety of reasons. Among the contributing factors include the adolescent's desire to seek relief from a difficult home situation, a belief that the baby will offer love and attention, a view that pregnancy reflects a rite of passage into adulthood, and a sense of hopelessness and despair about the future.

Self-esteem has often been cited as another major variable in decision making about pregnancy, and the majority of the prevention programs include self-esteem building as a major part of the curriculum. In the past five years, a wealth of so-called life planning or career development programs have been implemented in hopes that a teen's ability to select and plan career options will affect her/his decision to become sexually involved or to effectively use contraception.

Other explanations for unintended adolescent pregnancy relate to the level of cognitive development in adolescents. Such discussions encourage the development of programs to reach individuals who cannot think abstractly. This relates directly to one's ability to plan and realize the consequences of one's decisions and actions. Many adolescents believe they are invulnerable and are involved in risk-taking behaviors such as sexual activity, drinking, drugs, and malicious acts, which indicate the belief that "nothing can happen to me."[17]

A variety of programs have been developed in an attempt to prevent unintended adolescent pregnancy and parenting. In the area of prevention, many school-based programs include peer education/counseling models and direct educational programming. The consensus of the research in the field favors an integrated curricula in family life/human sexuality education beginning in kindergarten and continuing through the 12th grade. Educational interventions in community settings, including youth organizations, such as Boy's and Girl's Clubs, YMCAs, YWCAs, Scouts, and church groups have traditionally provided innovative approaches through weekend retreats, youth leadership training, peer education, and individual and group counseling. In addition, many community agencies across the country provide parent education to help parents communicate more effectively with their children about human sexuality.[18]

In our community, parent training is currently being provided to parents of preschool age children by the ABC Agency, the Parenting League, the North Grant City Community College District, and the Center for Family Well-Being. Other agencies in our community have targeted high school students for family life educational programs. To the best of our knowledge, our agency is the only one targeting the junior-high-school-age youth and their parents. We feel that intervention with this age group and their parents will be most effective in reducing unintended adolescent pregnancy.[19]

NEEDS STATEMENT CRITIQUE

(12) This is a strong introduction that places the problem in some national perspective.

(13) Because public figures on the poverty level of a community are easily obtainable, the argument could be strengthened by providing such information (e.g., 38% of the residents are living 200% below the poverty level and the average family income in the city is $15,000).

(14) Good depiction of the racial-ethnic and household composition of the community.

(15) What survey, conducted when, and by whom? Many times proposal writers will give data without the sources.

(16) More recent comparison data should also be provided that depicts the growing magnitude of the problem.

(17) These three paragraphs accomplish two important things in a need statement: They summarize the literature on the subject and they provide the reviewer with a broad perspective of the problem by identifying several contributing factors. However, the writer has failed to use the literature to support the need for the particular intervention proposed. Are you able to discern from these three paragraphs that the writer is proposing parent education training? When possible, it is vital that the literature be used as a rationale to support your proposal idea.

(18) This paragraph provides the reviewer with a good overview of the general approaches being taken to address the problem, but provides little information about their overall effectiveness.

(19) These statements reflect that the grantwriter is aware of what is specifically being done in the local community and can also identify the gaps in service. This helps to strengthen the request for support of the intervention.

In general, this need statement has not adequately identified the target group. While parent education is the proposed intervention, there is not sufficient evidence that it is an effective strategy for addressing the problem. There was little verification of the effectiveness of such an approach or how this approach is connected to the problem.

GOALS AND OBJECTIVES

SAMPLE PROPOSAL INSTRUCTIONS

Clearly describe the goals and objectives of the proposed project. State what you expect to accomplish during the project year. Indicate the degree of knowledge, attitude, or behavior change the target group will demonstrate by the end of the project.

Project Goals[20]

(1) To promote parental involvement with their adolescent children.

(2) To support and sustain the efforts of parents as the primary sexuality educators of their children.

(3) To increase parents' and children's knowledge related to human sexuality, adolescent development, and family dynamics.

(4) To facilitate access to health, educational, and social services related to prevention and care services.

Outcome Objectives[21]

(1) One hundred parents attending the Parenting Education Seminars will increase their knowledge about human sexuality and adolescent development.

(2) Fifty parents will spend a minimum of two hours per week in direct communication with their children about their values and knowledge related to sexuality, family, and interpersonal relationships.

(3) Fifty adolescents will be able to identify at least five advantages of sexual abstinence during adolescence.

(4) Fifty parents will increase by 60% their knowledge of community agencies providing contraceptive information, youth programs, and family life services.

(5) Fifty adolescents will increase their understanding of their parents' attitudes toward family life and values.

GOALS AND OBJECTIVES CRITIQUE

(20) These goals represent broad aims of the program and provide a general focus to the project.

(21) In contrast, the outcome objectives indicate measurable accomplishments expected during the funding period. They reflect specific behavioral

and knowledge changes desired of each target group; they do not describe the methods.

PROJECT ACTIVITIES

SAMPLE PROPOSAL INSTRUCTIONS

> Describe the major activities that will accomplish the project's objectives. Present implementation plans that describe what efforts will be taken to address the problems identified.

Introduction

The Geta Grant Agency is proposing to address the problem of unintended adolescent pregnancy in the community through two approaches: (1) parent education seminars and (2) parent-child "Let's Talk" sessions. These approaches acknowledge and support the parents as primary human sexuality educators of their children and will provide them with a structured opportunity to broach the subject with their adolescent children.[22]

Staffing Plans

The Parent Education Seminars will be organized and conducted by the Family Life Education Specialist, who has had extensive experience in conducting human sexuality workshops for both parents and students. Staff from other youth-serving community agencies will also serve as presenters.[23]

Parent and Youth Recruitment

Parents will be recruited through existing agency contacts in schools, churches, PTAs, voluntary associations, and community centers. Twenty-five parents will be recruited for each six-week seminar, or a total of 125 parents will become acquainted with the materials at the end of five six-week seminars.[24] Parents will be determined eligible for services if they meet four criteria:

(1) have children who are in the 6th, 7th, or 8th grade;

(2) agree to participate in the six-week parenting seminar, as well as complete the project evaluation component;

(3) agree to allow their children to participate in a six-week Family Life Education series and to complete the project evaluation component; and

(4) agree to sign, along with their children, a cooperative agreement indicating that they will spend a minimum of two hours per week working together on the *In the Know* workbook and/or videotape.[25]

Parent Education Curriculum

The curriculum for the Parent Education Seminars will consist of six major units. Each unit will have two sections: information for parents, and talking with your child. The six units include: (1) adolescent development, (2) understanding your body and human sexuality, (3) peer pressure, (4) self-image, (5) communicating effectively, and (6) effective decision making.[26]

Parent Education Seminars

Each Parent Education Seminar will consist of a once-a-week, two-hour session in the evenings for six weeks. A total of five seminars will be conducted during the funding period. The seminars will be held at five separate locations across the city to make them more accessible to parents. Permission to use the different facilities has already been obtained.

The presenters will use a variety of teaching strategies and materials, including videotapes, films, role playing, lecture, and discussion. Parents will be given easy-to-read handouts that cover each unit and contain helpful hints on discussing the subject with their children. A resource listing of other community agencies providing health care, including contraceptive information, mental health services, and youth programs, will be distributed to parents. These materials will be printed in English, Spanish, and Vietnamese.[27]

Parent-Child Communication Activities

At the end of each session of the Parent Education Seminar, the participants will be asked to spend at least two hours the following week discussing the subject with their children. To initiate and facilitate the parent-child communication process, parents will be asked to work with their children in reviewing a section each week in the *In the Know* workbook and/or videotape, which has been specifically designed for adolescents for understanding human sexuality and family life issues. Each section in the workbook and on the videotape coincides with the units presented in the parent seminars. Thus parents will be familiar with the subject matter before discussing it with their children and will have been provided with helpful hints on communicating with their children about the topic.[28]

This format will help parents to feel comfortable in talking with their children about human sexuality and family life and will also increase the opportunity for parents to share their own values and attitudes about a variety of subjects. In addition, parents will gain an understanding of their children's own views. Both parents and adolescents will be asked to provide feedback, criticisms, comments, and suggestions for improvement of the materials with which they are working. The desire for an assessment of the materials is not only useful for measuring project objectives, but will also provide adolescents with a rationale for discussing the subject matter with their parents.

Through the seminars, we will identify parents to serve as presenters. They will be asked to share their own experiences and strategies in using the materials with their children and to play a supportive role with other parents who may feel uncomfortable about exploring the subject matter with their children.

Research has shown that positive and effective parent-child communication about human sexuality are important factors in reducing unintended adolescent pregnancy. This proposed program will enhance parents' desire to discuss important issues facing our young people today.[29]

PROJECT ACTIVITIES CRITIQUE

(22) This introduction summarizes the major project activities and provides a rationale for their selection. This is helpful to the reviewer for it gives a framework for understanding the implementation plans.

(23) This is a limited staffing plan. It refers to staff being used from other agencies, yet there is no evidence (e.g., letters of support in the appendix) that such arrangements have been agreed upon. Including résumés of key project staff in the appendix is also important.

(24) Many times funders desire to see letter of cooperation from other agencies that will be involved in the project. If those are unavailable, the grantwriter can at least provide a listing of the agencies that will be contacted.

(25) These are clear indications of the target group and the eligibility criteria; however, there is no reference to any fee-for-service, which many funders wish to have addressed.

(26) Because curriculum development will be a major activity of the project, there should be greater delineation of the anticipated content of each unit (e.g., learning objectives, sample unit outline, teaching strategies, learning exercises). While funding will allow you to fully develop the curriculum, prospective funders need to gain confidence from the proposal that the activities planned can accomplish the project's objectives. The limited dis-

cussion in this proposal suggests that there has been little thought given to a major component of the project.

(27) Similarly, the proposal could be strengthened by a discussion of the seminar format and content (e.g., providing a typical seminar schedule, a listing of films, videotapes, and the like).

(28) There has been no discussion about the development of a workbook or videotape. Have they already been developed? If so, indicate their availability to the project. If not, what resources will be used for their production and/or distribution?

(29) These concluding paragraphs provide a sound rationale for the planned activities and help to generate confidence that the agency will successfully address the problem.

EVALUATION

SAMPLE PROPOSAL INSTRUCTIONS

> Identify the kinds of data to be collected and maintained and discuss the criteria to be used to evaluate the results and successes of the project. Indicate how the objectives will be measured to determine if they have been successfully accomplished.

The Parent Education Seminars and the *In the Know* workbook and/or videotape for parent-child activity are an innovative and unique concept to provide parents and their children not only with knowledge related to human sexuality, but with a *reason* to communicate with each other in sensitive topic areas. This project will increase knowledge and affect parent and child behaviors. Parents and their children will be asked to participate in the evaluation of the educational materials as well as in an evaluation of the overall project.

The Grant University Family Life Research Center will conduct the evaluation of this project (see Appendix for Letter of Agreement between the agency and Grant University and the principal investigator's curriculum vitae). There will be a two-part evaluation: First, an evaluation of the seminar content, materials, style, and method of presentation, and the parent-child *In the Know* workbook and/or videotape; and second, an overall evaluation of the impact on knowledge gained and behavioral change.

The five outcome objectives delineated in an earlier proposal section will serve as a basis for the second part of the evaluation. In general, we hypothesize that:

(1) as a result of the intervention, there will be an increase in the number and length of discussions between parents and children related to family values and human reproduction;

(2) as a result of the intervention, there will be an increase in the amount of direct questioning of children by parents related to the child's behavior and knowledge; and

(3) as a result of the intervention, children will pose more questions to their parents related to family values, attitudes, and beliefs.

Both parents and their children will be tested before and after the seminars, using questionnaires developed under this grant. In addition, parents will be asked to keep a diary during the course of the six-week seminar to record the nature of their interaction with their children. A matched comparison group of parents will be selected through local schools and parent groups to ascertain whether there are differences between them and those participating in the parenting seminars.[30]

EVALUATION CRITIQUE

(30) The agency plans to contract with a local university to provide evaluation assistance. A letter of agreement between the agency and an outsider evaluator is typically found in the appendix. Often proposal writers provide only a minimal discussion of the project evaluation, especially if an outside evaluation is planned. However, it is advisable to check with prospective funders before submitting the proposal to discern how detailed the plan for the evaluation should be. Though the evaluation design in this sample proposal is limited, there is some indication of: (1) the research hypotheses, (2) what will be measured, (3) who will be tested, (4) when and how the data will be collected, and (5) the type of design. A more detailed discussion would elaborate upon each of these facets of an evaluation as well as provide sample data collection instruments.

TABLE A.1 TIME LINE[31]

ACTIVITIES	MONTHS											
	1	2	3	4	5	6	7	8	9	10	11	12
	1st Quarter				*2nd Quarter*			*3rd Quarter*			*4th Quarter*	
Develop seminar curriculum and parent-child workbook and video	▬	▬	▬	▬								
Prepare evaluation plan					▬							
Schedule seminars and presenters					▬							
Review and finalize seminar materials and parent-child workbook and video						▬	▬					
Recruitment of parents and adolescents					▬	▬	▬	▬				
Preseminar evaluation						▬						
Conduct seminar and parent-child communication activities							▬	▬	▬	▬	▬	▬
Postseminar evaluation											▬	
Prepare final report												▬

TIME LINE CRITIQUE

(31) The time line reflects when the major activities of the project are to be accomplished. Note that the project evaluation is also included. Some funders may require a different time line format. Be sure to follow the proposal guidelines when developing it.

COMMUNITY REVIEW

If time permits, once a draft of a proposal is written, it can be beneficial to obtain community input. Other agency staff and/or community representatives can be invited to act as a review team in order to critique the proposal prior to submission. This helps to foster commitment and support for the project as well as helps to identify potential service delivery problems.

APPENDIX C: FUNDING RESOURCE INFORMATION

Listed below are common sources of information on funding resources that you might find helpful. This is a selective listing: for a more complete picture of funding opportunities, you can consult your local library, or contact one of the following organizations.

ORGANIZATIONS

The Grantsmanship Center
650 S. Spring Street, #507
Los Angeles, CA 90014

An organization that has an extensive inventory of funding information, it publishes a newspaper for grant-seeking organizations, and conducts national training on proposal writing and other areas of human service administration.

The Foundation Center
79 Fifth Avenue
New York, NY 10003

An independent, national service organization established by foundations to provide an authoritative source of information on private philanthropic giving, it publishes various directories and guides on foundations, and has established a national network of reference collections through local and university libraries, community foundations, and nonprofit organizations.

MAJOR PUBLICATIONS

Annual Register of Grant Support
Marquis Who's Who
4300 West 62nd Street
Indianapolis, IN 46206

Catalog of Federal Domestic Assistance
Superintendent of Documents
U.S. Government Printing Office
Washington, DC 20402

Federal Grants and Contracts Weekly
Capitol Publications
1300 North 17th Street
Arlington, VA 22209

Federal Register
Superintendent of Documents
U.S. Government Printing Office
Washington, DC 20402

Foundation Directory, Foundation Directory Supplements, Foundation Grants Index, National Data Book of Foundations, Corporate Foundation Profiles
Publications of the Foundation Center
79 Fifth Avenue
New York, NY 10003

Fund Raiser's Guide to Human Service Funding (2nd ed.)
The Taft Group
5130 MacArthur Blvd., N.W.
Washington, DC 20016-3316

Grantsmanship Book
Reprints from the Grantsmanship Center
650 S. Spring Street #507
Los Angeles, CA 90014

(See Lauffer 1983, pp. 65-67 for a guide on developing a foundation funding source inventory.)

COMPUTERIZED SEARCHES AND DATA BASES

There are a number of computerized search services available that provide funding resource information. The advantage of such data bases is that they can subdivide and index the funding information into a range of subjects and categories (e.g., by subject or by geographic area). The costs can vary and some of the information overlaps in the different data bases. Check your library for more information about search services.

DIALOG Information Retrieval Service is among the largest data bases, with more than 320 data sources, covering a broad range of topics. Among the funding-related data bases in the service are the following:

Federal Index
Federal Register Abstracts
Federal Research in Progress
Foundation Directory
Foundation Grants Index
Grants
National Foundations

Computerized searches are also useful for readily identifying literature and data for the needs/problem statement section of the proposal.

REFERENCES AND SUGGESTIONS FOR FURTHER READING

Brindis, C., & Reyes, P. B. (1988). *Evaluating your information and education project.* San Francisco: University of California, Center for Population and Reproductive Health Policy Institute for Health Policy Studies.

Bryce, H. J. (1987). *Financial and strategic management for nonprofit organizations.* Englewood Cliffs, NJ: Prentice-Hall.

Conrad, D. L. (1980). *The quick proposal workbook.* San Francisco: Public Management Institute.

Demone, H. W., & Gibelman, M. (Eds.). (1989). *Services for sale.* New Brunswick, NJ: Rutgers University Press.

Dryfoos, J.G. (1984). A new strategy for preventing unintended teenage childbearing. *Family Planning Perspectives,* 16(4), 193-195.

Guttmacher Institute. (1981). *Teenage pregnancy—the problem that hasn't gone away.* New York, NY: Author.

Hall, M. (1988). *Getting funded: A complete guide to proposal writing* (3rd ed.). Portland, OR: Continuing Education Publications.

Highlights from Council on Foundations Convention. (1988). *The Grantsmanship Center Whole Nonprofit Catalog, (Summer),* p. 26.

Kettner, P. M., & Martin, L. L. (1985). Generating competition in the human services through purchase of service contracting. In D. L. Thompson (Ed.), *The private exercise of public functions.* Port Washington: Associated Faculty Press.

Kettner, P. M., & Martin, L. L. (1987). *Purchase of service contracting.* Newbury Park, CA: Sage.

Kiritz, N. J. (1980). *Program planning and proposal writing.* Los Angeles: Grantsmanship Center.

Lauffer, A. (1983). *Grantsmanship* (2nd ed.). Beverly Hills, CA: Sage.

Lauffer, A. (1984). *Grantsmanship and fundraising.* Beverly Hills, CA: Sage.

Lefferts, R. (1982). *Getting a grant in the 1980's* (2nd ed.). Englewood Cliffs, NJ: Prentice-Hall.

Mack, K., & Skjei, E. (1979). *Overcoming writing blocks.* Los Angeles: J. P. Tarcher.

Morris, L. L., & Fitz-Gibbon, C. T. (1978). *How to deal with goals and objectives.* Beverly Hills, CA: Sage.

Morris, L. L., & Fitz-Gibbon, C. T. (1978). *How to measure program implementation.* Beverly Hills, CA: Sage.

Morris, L. L., & Fitz-Gibbon, C. T. (1978). *How to design a program evaluation.* Beverly Hills, CA: Sage.

National Institute of Mental Health. (1976). *A working manual of simple program evaluation techniques for community mental health centers.* Washington, DC: Government Printing Office.

Pecora, P. J., & Austin, M. J. (1987). *Managing human services personnel*. Newbury Park, CA: Sage.

Schaefer, M. (1985). *Designing and implementing procedures for health and human services*. Beverly Hills, CA: Sage.

Schaefer, M. (1987). *Implementing change in service programs*. Newbury Park, CA: Sage.

Shakely, J. (1986, February). Adolescent pregnancy in Los Angeles: A call for cooperative action. *Panel Presentation at the Los Angeles County Adolescent Pregnancy Childbirth Conference*. Los Angeles.

Sultz, H. A., & Sherwin, F. S. (1981). *Grant writing for health professionals*. Boston: Little, Brown.

Tarshis, B. (1985). *How to write without pain*. New York: Plume.

Townsend, T. H. (1974). Criteria grantors use in assessing proposals. *Foundation news, 15*(2), 33-38.

Tringo, J. (1982). Learning from failure: Resubmitting your rejected proposal. *Grants Magazine, 5*(1), 18-22.

Tripodi, T. (1983). *Evaluative research for social workers*. Englewood Cliffs, NJ: Prentice-Hall.

Vinter, R. D., & Kish, R. K. (1984). *Budgeting for not-for-profit organizations*. New York: Free Press.

Wacht, R. F. (1984). *Financial management in non-profit organizations*. Atlanta: Georgia State University.

Weiss, C. H. (1972). *Evaluation research*. Englewood Cliffs, NJ: Prentice-Hall.

York, R. O. (1982). *Human service planning*. Chapel Hill: University of North Carolina Press.

ABOUT THE AUTHORS

Soraya M. Coley, Ph.D., Professor of Human Services at California State University, Fullerton, has taught program design and proposal writing, and research for the past 15 years. She is also President of Colemoore & Associates, a human services consulting and training group that provides technical assistance and training on grantsmanship and program evaluation to public and private human service agencies. Dr. Coley serves on grant and contract review panels at the local and federal levels. She completed a Postdoctoral Fellowship at the Institute for Social Research, University of Michigan. Previously she directed a federally funded national project on child abuse prevention and has served as project manager for several national research projects. Dr. Coley is the author of several research reports, and has contributed to journals such as *Social Casework, Journal of Counseling and Development, Journal of Counseling and Human Service Professions,* and *Journal of Gerontological Social Work.*

Cynthia A. Scheinberg is the Executive Director of the Coalition for Children, Adolscents and Parents in Orange, California and has a master's degree in cultural anthropology and is working on her Ph.D. in clinical psychology at Pacifica Graduate Institute in Santa Barbara, California. She is a successful grantwriter, having received support from both public and private funders for a nonprofit human service agency she directs. She has taught proposal writing in the Human Services Program, California State University, Fullerton, and has served as chairperson and president of both statewide and local organizations. She consults with numerous community organizations on coalition building and proposal writing.